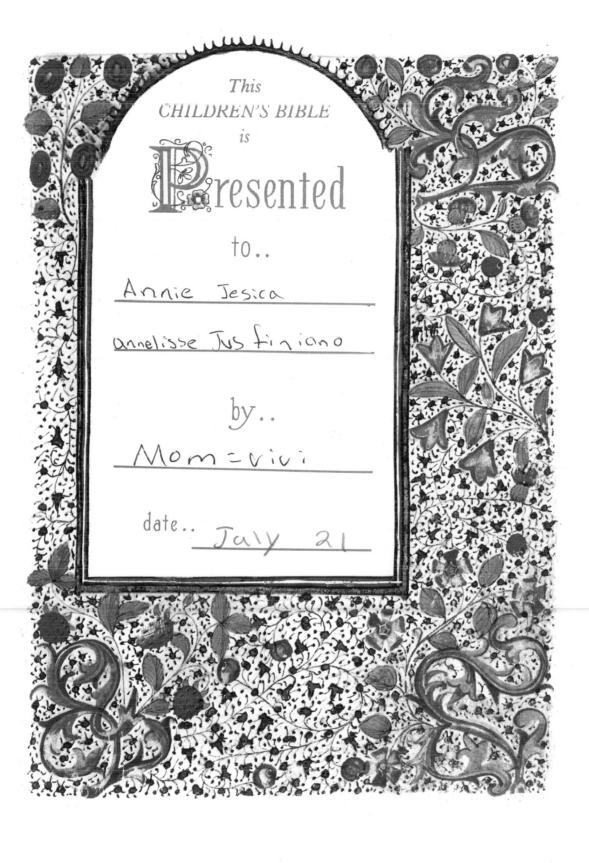

This
CHILDREN'S BIBLE
is

Presented

to..

Annie Jesica

annelisse Jusfiniano

by..

Mom = vivi

date.. July 21

"In the past God spoke to our ancestors [in the Old Testament] in partial and various ways through the Prophets.

"In these latter days, God spoke to us [in the New Testament] through His Son."
—Hebrews 1:1-2

SAINT JOSEPH
ILLUSTRATED
CHILDREN'S BIBLE

POPULAR STORIES FROM THE
OLD AND NEW TESTAMENTS

By
REV. JUDE WINKLER, O.F.M. Conv.

ILLUSTRATED IN FULL COLOR

CATHOLIC BOOK PUBLISHING CO.
New York

FOREWORD

I REMEMBER well the first time that I tried to read the Bible. It was a large book with many strange names. I opened it up to the first page and started reading.

By the time I reached the end of the third page, I realized that this was probably hopeless, because there were too many things that I just did not understand. It took me a long time before I found the courage to give it another go.

As I write this book, I am hopeful that it might save someone from that experience. The beautiful illustrations in this book will help you to picture what was going on when these stories took place. I have retold the Bible stories in a way that I hope will make them easy to understand. I have also attempted to keep the strange names of the people and places to an absolute minimum.

When you read this book, you will notice that the language I use is drawn from the Bible itself. I have used as many phrases and images from the Bible as I could so that when one starts to read the Bible itself, the stories will be very familiar.

May the Holy Spirit be with you as you read this book.

Imprimi Potest: Daniel Pietrzak, OFM Conv., Minister Provincial of St. Anthony of Padua Province (USA)
Nihil Obstat: James T. O'Connor, S.T.D., Censor Librorum
Imprimatur: ✠ **Patrick J. Sheridan, D.D.,** Vicar General, Archdiocese of New York

The Nihil Obstat and Imprimatur are official declarations that a book or pamphlet is free of doctrinal or moral error. No implication is contained therein that those who have granted the Nihil Obstat and Imprimatur agree with the contents, opinions or statements expressed.

T-635

7 8 9 10 11 12 13 14 15

CONTENTS

The New Testament

THE OLD TESTAMENT

ALL throughout the pages of the Old Testament, we meet a God who is so filled with love that He reaches out to His people again and again.

The first pages of the Old Testament tell us what happened at the beginning of the world. God created the world and all that is in it. He called Adam and Eve to live in His happiness, but they rebelled against Him. God then called a holy people through Abraham and Sarah.

He protected them against their enemies. He saved them from their slavery in Egypt through Moses. He made them a mighty nation with David as their king. And, most important of all, He made a holy covenant with them that He would always be their God and they would always be His people.

Even when His people turned away from Him, God did not stop loving them. He punished them so that they would turn from their sins and turn back to Him. He sent them prophets who taught them the ways of the Lord. He led them back from exile to the promised land.

The final pages of the Old Testament show that God's love is far beyond what we would expect. He promised His people that He would send a chosen one to call them out of their slavery to sin. He prepared them for the day when He would send His only Son, Jesus, into our world.

GOD CREATES THE WORLD

Genesis 1:1-25

LONG before there was anything in the heavens, on the earth, or under the earth, God was filled with love. God the Father, the Son, and the Holy Spirit was so filled with love that He wanted to share this love with someone. And so He decided to create the world and all that is in it.

On the first day God said, "Let there be light," and there was light. God saw that the light was good. He separated the light from darkness, calling the light day and the darkness night.

On the second day God made an opening in the waters. He pushed the waters aside and made a space, which He called the heavens. There were waters above the heavens and below the heavens, but in the heavens there was no water.

Then on the third day God separated the waters from the dry land. He called the dry land earth and the waters He called the sea. These, too, were good.

So God called forth all kinds of plants upon the earth. There were all types of plants that had seeds and there were those which had fruit with the seeds in them. God saw that this, too, was good.

On the fourth day God created the lights in the sky. These lights would help us to mark out the seasons and the days and the months and the years. They would also give light to the earth during the day and during the night.

That fourth day God made the stars and the two great lights which light up the heavens. The larger light was the sun, which gave light during the day. The smaller light was the moon and it gave light during the night. The sun and the moon and all the stars were very good.

On the fifth day God created the animals that live in the sea and those that live in the skies. He created the fish and the whales, the birds and the insects. God blessed these animals and told them to multiply and fill the earth. All these animals were very good.

On the morning of the sixth day God created all the animals that live upon the earth. He created those that live in the forests and those that live on the farms. There were bears and snakes, cows and sheep, and all kinds of animals. These animals were all very good, but God was still not finished. God wanted to share His life and His love with us.

God creates all the plants on the earth.

The serpent tempts Adam and Eve.

ADAM AND EVE

Genesis 1:26—4:16

AND so later on the sixth day God took some dust from the earth, He formed it into the shape of a man, and He breathed His Spirit into the man. He named this first man Adam.

God loved Adam very much, and He put him in a beautiful garden called the Garden of Eden. In the middle of the garden there were two special trees: the tree of life and the tree of the knowledge of good and evil. He told Adam that he could eat of the fruit of any of the trees in the garden, but he was not supposed to eat the fruit of the tree of the knowledge of good and evil that was in the middle of the garden.

God had Adam give names to all the animals that were in the garden. Whatever Adam named an animal, that was what it would be called.

But God saw that Adam was not happy for he was all alone. So God caused Adam to fall into a deep sleep. While he was asleep, God took a rib out of his side. He used the rib to form the first woman, Eve.

When Adam saw Eve, he was very pleased. God blessed them and told them that they should have many children. Adam and Eve were very happy living in the Garden of Eden.

One day, as Eve was walking in the garden, a serpent spoke to her. It wanted to tempt her and her husband to sin. The serpent asked her whether it was true that God had told them that they could not eat the fruit of the tree of knowledge of good and evil. He continued to tempt Eve and told her that God would not let her eat of this tree because He knew that if Adam and Eve ate of the fruit, then they would become like God. The serpent wanted to make Eve jealous.

Eve took some of the fruit and ate it. Then she gave some of it to Adam, and he also ate it. As soon as they ate the fruit, they realized that they had sinned, and they were ashamed.

That evening they heard God walking in the garden, and they hid from Him. God called out and asked them why they were hiding. He knew that they had sinned, and now He had to punish them.

God ordered Adam and Eve to leave the garden. He placed two angels at the gate of the garden to prevent them from ever coming back. They would have to work hard and suffer much because of their sin. The serpent, too, was punished for it lost its legs and had to crawl on its belly the rest of its days.

Yet even then God continued to love Adam and Eve. He showed His love for them by making some clothes for them to protect them from the heat and the cold.

Adam and Eve had two sons. The older son was named Cain, and the younger son was named Abel. Cain was a farmer, and Abel was a shepherd.

One day each of them offered a sacrifice to God. God accepted the sacrifice offered by Abel but not that offered by Cain. This made Cain very jealous and angry, so he took his brother out into the field and he killed him. When God asked Cain where Abel his brother was, Cain answered, "I am not my brother's keeper."

God punished Cain for this very evil sin by making him wander over the earth. He would no longer have any place that he could call his home. Yet, even then, God showed His love for Cain by putting a mark on his forehead so that no one would harm him.

The waters of the flood cover the entire earth.

GOD DECIDES TO PUNISH THE EARTH

Genesis 6:5—7:24

THE sin that started with Adam and Eve continued to grow worse and worse. Even the horrible thing that Cain had done when he killed his own brother was only the beginning. More and more men and women sinned and did whatever God had told them not to do.

The world became so sinful that God decided that things had to change. He could not sit by while people were hurting each other and while they were openly disobeying what He had told them to do. He warned them over and over again, but they just would not listen to Him.

And so God decided that He would destroy the world and begin again. He would send a great flood over all the earth to kill every living thing. The flood would be so great that there would not be a single place, not even the highest hills and mountains, that would not be covered by water.

Yet, there was one family that obeyed God: the family of Noah. God decided that He would save Noah, his wife, their sons and their daughters-in-law from the flood.

God spoke to Noah and told him that He intended to destroy all life upon the earth but that He would save him and his family.

He ordered Noah to build a great boat, an Ark, about 450 feet long, 75 feet wide, and 45 feet high. When the boat was finished, Noah and his family were to gather animals of every kind and lead them on board.

This way, even though there was destruction all over the earth, none of the type of animals that God had created would be lost.

Noah and his sons immediately began to build the boat that God had commanded them to build. Noah's wife and his sons' wives began to prepare all the food that they would need for this long journey.

All of Noah's neighbors must have been wondering what he was doing. They probably made fun of him and called him all kinds of names. Yet they did not stop sinning.

Then the day came when Noah and his family had finished all their work. They gathered all the animals into the boat and closed all its doors and windows. Just then, it began to rain. It rained harder than it had ever rained before. It seemed as if the very windows of the heavens had opened. But the people on the earth still kept sinning.

After a while, the rivers and lakes could no longer hold all the waters. They began to overflow more and more. At first the people thought this was just a normal flood like those that often happened during the spring. But the rain just did not stop. And the people kept on sinning.

The rain was so hard that it began to flood in places where it had never flooded before. The people ran to the high ground, but soon even that was covered. Soon even the highest mountains were covered. There was not a dry place on the earth.

Every person and every animal that was upon the earth lost their lives in the flood. But Noah and his family were safe in the Ark.

Even after all the mountains were covered by the flood, it continued to rain. In all, it rained for forty days and forty nights. And the water just kept rising.

God blesses Noah and all living creatures.

A COVENANT WITH NOAH

Genesis 8:1—11:9

THEN, after it had rained for forty days and forty nights, it stopped raining. The water slowly began to recede, but it took a long, long time before all the water had gone away. Eventually, the Ark came to rest on the top of a very high mountain, Mount Ararat.

After forty days, Noah opened one of the windows of the Ark. He released a raven to see if the water had gone down enough. It flew back and forth, looking for dry land, but it was still too early.

He then released a dove, but it could not find any place to land, so it returned to the Ark. Noah thus knew that it was not yet safe to get off the Ark.

God spoke again to Noah and told him it was now time for him and his family to get off the Ark. They opened the doors and they all got out.

As soon as Noah left the Ark, he offered a sacrifice to thank God for protecting him and his family. This pleased God very much.

And so God made a promise to Noah and to all people upon the earth. He promised that He would never again destroy the earth with a flood. Promises such as these are called covenants. God gave Noah and us a reminder of this covenant: the rainbow.

Every time we look into the sky and see a rainbow, we can remember how much God loves us and how He made this special covenant with Noah and with us.

Having seen the great power of God and also His great mercy, men and women should have decided to follow God with all their heart and soul. But almost immediately they began to sin again.

Noah planted a garden and grew grapes in it. He made some juice from the grapes and let the juice sit for a few days before he drank it.

The juice turned into wine, and when Noah drank it he became very drunk. He did not know that this would happen, for this was the first time that anyone had ever tasted wine.

Noah fell asleep in his tent, and his sons entered the tent and one of them made fun of him. Noah punished the son for his disrespect, for he had sinned against God and against him.

Later, the people on the earth decided to build a great tower, the tower of Babel, to try to reach the heavens for they wanted to be like God. This was something that greatly displeased God. He punished those who had built the tower by making them each speak a different language so that they could no longer understand each other.

God leads Abraham to the promised land.

GOD CALLS ABRAHAM AND SARAH

Genesis 12:1—17:27

GOD now knew that He would have to follow a different plan. Up to this time, He had called all the people on earth to follow Him. But time after time they had turned away from Him and had sinned. Now He would call one man and one woman, Abraham and Sarah, who would be the father and mother of a new people.

Abram, for this was his name at the time, lived in the city of Ur where the people believed in many gods. The Lord called Abram and told him to leave his home and all those whom he knew. He was to take his family and travel to the land that God would show him.

So Abram gathered his wife, his cousin Lot, their families, and all that they owned. They set off to follow God's call.

They traveled a great distance until they reached the land of Israel. This was the land that God had promised to give to Abram and his descendants, but almost immediately there was a problem.

The land of Israel was suffering from a great famine, so Abram and Sarai had to travel to Egypt to find some food to eat so that they would not die.

When they arrived in Egypt, Abram became frightened for he realized that Sarai, his wife, was beautiful. He feared that the king, the Pharaoh, would kill him in order to steal her. So Abram told everyone that Sarai was his sister. But God protected Sarai and Abram and they were able to leave Egypt in safety.

God blessed Abram and Lot and they became so rich that they decided that it would be better for them to go their separate ways. This would keep their shepherds from fighting with each other at the watering holes. Abram was older than Lot and he could have ordered Lot to go wherever he said, but he was so generous that he let Lot choose first. Lot went off to the south, taking the best land for himself.

God blessed Abram for his generosity. He visited Abram one evening and told him to look up into the sky. God told Abram that he would have as many descendants as there were stars in the sky.

Abram prepared a sacrifice, and God made a most sacred covenant with Abram. He promised Abram that his son and grandson would inherit the land in which they were living.

But Sarai still did not have any children. And so one day Sarai sent her servant, Hagar, into Abram's tent so that she could have a child. Sarai planned to adopt Hagar's son when he was born.

Hagar had a son whom she named Ishmael. He was a strong and handsome boy, but he was not going to inherit the promise. God told Abram again that He would make him the father of many nations.

God also told Abram that his name from then on would be Abraham and Sarai's name would be Sarah. God promised them that they would have a son whom they would name Isaac. He was to be the child of the promise.

Abraham trusted in the promise that God had made to them. He, for his part, committed himself to this covenant. He had himself and all the males in his camp circumcised, for this was a sign of the covenant that they had made with God.

But still he and Sarah did not have any children, and they continued to wait for the Lord to fulfill the promise that He had made to them.

Abraham prepares a meal for the Lord.

GOD VISITS ABRAHAM AND SARAH

Genesis 18:1—19:38

THEN one day Abraham was standing outside his tent when he saw three strangers passing by. He realized that they might be hungry for they were in the middle of the desert. So Abraham ran over to them and bowed down to the earth. He asked them to grace him with their stay, for he wished to offer them a bit of bread.

When the three strangers made themselves comfortable, he ran off to Sarah and told her to take some flour and to prepare bread for their guests. He brought some milk for his guests to drink and took one of his calves and had it prepared for their supper.

This whole time Abraham had not realized that his three guests were really God and two of His angels. Once again, Abraham had shown himself to be a very generous person, and God was very pleased with him.

God asked Abraham where Sarah his wife was. Abraham answered that she was in the tent. God told Abraham that she would surely give birth to a son by the time that He would pass by again the next year.

Sarah had been listening inside the tent while God and Abraham were talking. When she heard God tell Abraham that she would have a son, she burst out laughing, for she and Abraham were too old to have children. God heard her laugh and asked her why she did not trust in Him for nothing was impossible for God.

God was a good friend of Abraham, so He also told Abraham all about His plans. He told Abraham that He was sending two of His angels to the cities of Sodom and Gomorrah to destroy them for they were filled with sinners.

Abraham was disturbed by this, for Lot, his nephew, and Lot's family lived in Sodom. So Abraham asked God whether it was right for Him to destroy these cities if there were innocent people living there. What if, for example, there were fifty just people living there? God told Abraham that He would not destroy the cities if fifty just people were found there.

Abraham then lowered the number and God kept agreeing not to destroy the cities if even the lower number of just people were found there. Finally, Abraham and God agreed on the number of just ten good people, but there were not even ten good people in these cities. So God completely destroyed the cities, saving only Abraham's nephew, Lot, and his family.

The angel of the Lord saves Isaac's life.

GOD TESTS ABRAHAM

Genesis 21:1—22:19

THE Lord showed His great love for Abraham for He fulfilled the promise that He had made to Abraham and Sarah. In spite of the fact that both Abraham and Sarah were too old to have children, Sarah conceived and gave birth to a son.

Abraham and Sarah named their son Isaac. This name means laughter, for Isaac's birth brought great joy to Abraham and Sarah. They circumcised their son when he was eight days old, just as God had commanded them to do. All who had heard of the great things that the Lord had done for Abraham and Sarah rejoiced along with them.

Abraham now had two sons: Ishmael, the son of Hagar the slave, and Isaac, the son of Sarah. One day Sarah saw Ishmael outside with her son Isaac. She became frightened for she realized that Ishmael might harm her son in order to inherit Abraham's wealth. Sarah spoke to Abraham, asking him to send Ishmael away. Abraham was bothered by her request, but the Lord instructed him to do everything that Sarah asked of him.

The next morning Abraham sent Hagar and her son Ishmael away into the desert. He gave them a bit of bread and a skin of water. They soon ran out of water and Hagar was sure that she and her son would die of thirst. But God protected her and her son, for He led Hagar to a well in the desert. God was with Ishmael, and he grew into a strong and courageous warrior. He became the father of a line of kings.

Isaac, though, was the son of the promise that God had made to Abraham and Sarah. He continued to fill their hearts with joy.

One day God spoke to Abraham to test him. He called out and told Abraham that he should take his only son Isaac, whom he loved, to the land of Moriah. There he was to sacrifice Isaac to the Lord on the mountain that God would show him.

Abraham was terribly troubled by what the Lord had asked of him. Yet he obeyed. The next morning he rose early, prepared his donkeys, cut some wood, and left on his journey. He brought Isaac and two young men along with him.

On the third day of their journey, Abraham looked up and saw the place where he was to sacrifice his son. He told the two young men to remain at the base of the mountain while he and Isaac went up to perform their sacrifice. Isaac carried the wood while Abraham carried the knife and the fire.

As they were climbing the mountain, Isaac asked his father what they were going to sacrifice. Abraham responded that God would provide a sacrifice for them. When they reached the top of the mountain, Abraham built an altar upon which he would perform his sacrifice. He tied up his son and laid him upon the altar that he had built.

Abraham was ready to sacrifice his son and had lifted up his knife when he heard someone call his name. An angel was calling out to him to stop him from sacrificing his son. The angel told Abraham that God was very pleased with him for he had been willing to obey God in all things, even to the point of sacrificing his only son.

Looking up, Abraham saw a ram that was caught in a bush nearby. He took the ram and sacrificed it to the Lord. The angel spoke again to Abraham and told him that his descendants would be as numerous as the stars in the sky or the sand on the shore of the sea.

The servant finds Rebekah as a wife for Isaac.

ISAAC MARRIES REBEKAH

Genesis 23:1—24:67

SOON after this time, Sarah died and Abraham wept greatly for his beloved wife. He then went to speak to some of the people who lived in that land. He told them that he was a stranger in that land, but he asked their help in buying some land where he could bury his wife. They spoke in Abraham's behalf, and Abraham was able to buy a cave in the area we now call Hebron.

Abraham himself had grown very old, and he was concerned that he find a proper wife for his son. He did not want Isaac to marry any of the pagan women who lived in that land. Rather, he sent his servant to the land of his ancestors so that he might find a wife for Isaac and bring her back to marry him.

Abraham's servant took ten of his master's camels and packed them with all kinds of gifts. He traveled to the city of Nahor where Abraham's relatives lived. There he halted and waited outside of the city at the well, for the women of that place would come to the well each evening to draw water for their families. He prayed that God might give him a sign to tell him which woman was to marry Isaac.

He asked that the chosen woman offer water not only to him but to his camels as well.

As he was still speaking, Rebekah came out to get water for her family. Rebekah was beautiful and a very generous woman. Thus, when Abraham's servant went up to her and asked her for water, she immediately offered water both to him and to his camels. Abraham's servant then knew that she was the woman whom God had chosen to be Isaac's wife.

He took out a large gold ring and two arm bracelets and he gave them to her. She took him home, and there he spoke with her family. He asked them whether she might travel back with him to marry the son of his master.

Rebekah agreed to go with the servant and they traveled to the land where Abraham was living. One evening Isaac was out in the field when he saw some camels approaching from a distance, and he knew that it was the servant returning from his journey. Rebekah, likewise, saw Isaac from a distance and she prepared herself to meet him. Isaac and Rebekah fell in love with each other, for the Lord had blessed their marriage.

Jacob steals the blessing of Esau, his brother.

ISAAC AND HIS BLESSING

Genesis 25:19—27:29

FOR a long time, Isaac and Rebekah did not have any children. So Isaac prayed to the Lord, and God answered his prayers. Rebekah conceived and gave birth to twins.

Even while they were still in the womb, Rebekah's two children fought with each other. She asked the Lord why this was happening, and the Lord responded that they would be the fathers of two separate nations that would fight with each other.

The older son was named Esau, and he was a hunter. The younger son was named Jacob, and he was a shepherd.

Rebekah loved Jacob more than Esau. When Isaac had grown old, he told his son Esau to go hunting and to prepare a meal for him. Isaac promised Esau that when he had finished eating, he would give him his blessing.

But while Esau was out hunting, Rebekah dressed Jacob up so that he looked and smelled like Esau. Isaac was almost blind, so he smelled his son's clothes and they smelled like Esau's, and he felt his son's arms that were covered with fur, and they felt like Esau's arms. He was completely convinced that it was Esau kneeling before him, so he gave him his special blessing.

Jacob is visited by the Lord in a dream.

JACOB AND HIS DREAM

Genesis 27:30—28:22

WHEN Esau returned from his hunt, he found out what Jacob, his brother, had done. He was very angry and determined to get even with him. Rebekah, their mother, found out about this and warned Jacob. She told him to flee for his life and to travel to the land of their ancestors. There he would find safety.

Rebekah also told Jacob that he should not marry one of the women who lived in the land in which they were now dwelling. Instead, she told him to marry one of the women from their own family, which was dwelling in the land of their ancestors. While Jacob was traveling to the land of his ancestors, he stopped at the shrine of Bethel. There he fell asleep and dreamt that there was a ladder leading up into the heavens. There were angels going up and down the ladder. He heard God say that He was the Lord, the God of Abraham and the God of Isaac. God promised Jacob that He would give the land to him and his descendants. He also promised Jacob that he would have as many descendants as there are particles of dust on the earth.

Jacob woke up the next morning and thanked God for this special revelation. He then built an altar to celebrate God's love.

Jacob meets Rachel at the well.

JACOB MARRIES HIS BELOVED RACHEL

Genesis 29:1—35:19

JACOB then finished his journey to Haran, the land of his ancestors. When he reached that city, he stopped at the well where the sheep were watered. There was a large stone over the mouth of the well, so large that it would take many men to roll it back. Jacob saw a woman there who was very beautiful, Rachel. He was so moved by her beauty that he was able to roll the stone back all by himself.

Rachel brought Jacob back to her home where she introduced him to Laban, her uncle. Laban invited Jacob to stay with them and even to marry his niece.

Jacob worked for Laban for seven years in order to have the right to marry Rachel. After seven years of work, they held a wedding feast. The next morning when they awoke, Jacob realized that he had married Leah, Rachel's sister. He had been tricked.

Laban made Jacob work for another seven years for the right to marry Rachel (in those days one could have more than one wife). After he had married Rachel, Jacob continued to work for Laban and his family for a number of years. Laban promised Jacob a portion of the flock in return for the work he did.

Once again, Laban tried to cheat Jacob, for he would promise him those lambs which he was sure would be few and weak. But Jacob had learned the secrets of how to make sheep give birth to lambs and goats give birth to kids of a given color.

Thus, whenever Laban would promise Jacob a particular type of sheep or goat, all of the strong sheep and goats would give birth to lambs and kids of that color. Over the years, Jacob became very rich, and Laban and his family became jealous of him.

In the meantime, Leah had given birth to many children. Leah's servant and Rachel's servant also had many children, but Rachel did not have any children for a long time. Finally, Rachel gave birth first to Joseph and then to Benjamin, but she died giving birth to her second son.

Jacob eventually returned to the land that had been promised to Abraham, where he made peace with Esau, his brother.

JOSEPH AND HIS BROTHERS

Genesis 37:1—50:26

OF all the children whom Jacob had, he loved Joseph the most because he was the son of Rachel. He gave Joseph a special coat with many different colors as a sign of his love.

Joseph would have dreams in which his father and his brothers would bow down to him to give him honor. Joseph's brothers were jealous of the special love that Jacob had for him, and they were also jealous of the dreams.

One day while Joseph's brothers were out in the fields taking care of the flocks, Jacob sent Joseph to see how they were doing. Joseph's brothers saw him from a distance, and as he approached their camp, they plotted to harm him. They threw him into a well and they planned to kill him.

However, when the brothers saw some merchants passing by who were on their way to Egypt, they decided to sell Joseph to them as a slave. They then took Joseph's coat and covered it with blood so that Jacob would think that he had been killed by a wild animal.

God protected Joseph, even when he was a slave in Egypt. Joseph was sold to a man named Potiphar, who made him the head of his household. But Joseph got into trouble when Potiphar's wife accused him of doing evil things, so Potiphar had him thrown into prison.

While he was in prison, he met two of Pharaoh's servants who had been thrown into prison. He helped them by explaining the meaning of their dreams.

When Pharaoh had a dream that no one could explain, one of these servants who had since been set free remembered that Joseph could explain the meaning of dreams. So Joseph was called out of prison to explain Pharaoh's dream.

Pharaoh had dreamt that seven fat cows were eating by the Nile River when seven very thin cows came out of the river and ate the fat cows. Joseph explained that this dream meant that there would be seven years of plenty followed by seven years of famine.

Joseph told Pharaoh that he should appoint someone to collect grain during the years of plenty and then there would be enough to eat during the years of famine. So Pharaoh placed Joseph in charge of his entire kingdom.

When the famine began, the family of Joseph did not have enough food to eat. Joseph's father, Jacob, sent Joseph's brothers down to Egypt to buy food because he had heard that there was enough to eat there.

Joseph reveals who he is to his brothers.

The brothers journeyed to Egypt and came before Joseph to buy grain, but they did not recognize him. Joseph sold them grain but secretly returned their money to them.

Joseph also had one of the brothers thrown into prison until they would return with their youngest brother, Benjamin.

The brothers went home, but they were afraid to return to Egypt because they thought that Joseph might accuse them of stealing their money back. Finally, the famine became so bad that they had to go back to Egypt with their brother Benjamin.

When they arrived there, Joseph prepared a great meal for them. There he revealed that he was Joseph, their brother. He told them that he had forgiven them for all the things that they had done to him.

Joseph urged his brothers to go back to Israel to bring their father and all their families down to Egypt, for God would protect them there from the famine. The people of Israel lived in Egypt for over four hundred years.

The daughter of Pharaoh finds the baby Moses in the basket.

GOD PROTECTS THE BABY MOSES

Exodus 1:1—2:15

GOD blessed the people of Israel so much in these years that they grew to be very strong. There were so many of them that the people of Egypt began to fear them.

Pharaoh, the king of Egypt, made cruel laws to hurt the children of Israel. He commanded that all the baby boys of Israel be thrown into the Nile River.

At this time a certain mother and father of Israel had a son who was blessed by the Lord. They put him into a basket and placed the basket in the Nile River. The daughter of Pharaoh saw the basket and opened it up. When she saw that there was a baby boy inside the basket, she realized that he was a son of Israel. She decided to adopt the baby, and she named him Moses. She raised Moses as if he were her very own son.

When Moses had grown up, he went out one day and saw an Egyptian beating up a Jewish slave. He killed the Egyptian to protect the son of Israel. But Pharaoh came to know of what had happened, so Moses had to flee out into the desert.

God speaks to Moses from the burning bush.

THE BURNING BUSH

Exodus 2:15—4:31

MOSES fled to the land of Midian where he fell asleep near a well. Seven daughters of Jethro, a priest of Midian, came to water their flocks at that well, but they were chased away by some evil shepherds.

When Moses woke up, he chased the evil shepherds away. The daughters of Jethro were so grateful that they told their father about him. Jethro invited Moses to join their people and he cared for their flocks. He also married one of the daughters of Jethro, Zipporah, and they had two sons.

One day while Moses was out in the desert, he saw a strange sight on the mountain. He saw a bush that was on fire but which did not burn up. Moses climbed up the mountain to see what was happening.

God spoke to Moses from the bush. He told Moses that He was sending him to free His people from their slavery in Egypt.

God told Moses that if the people asked Moses who had sent him, he was to answer that "Yahweh" had sent him. "Yahweh" means, "I am who am."

Moses was frightened, but God told him to have courage for He would be with him. God also sent Aaron, Moses' brother, to be his spokesman.

The people of Israel pass through the Red Sea.

GOD FREES HIS PEOPLE

Exodus 5:1—14:1

MOSES and Aaron went to Pharaoh to ask him to let God's people go free, but Pharaoh would not listen to them.

So God sent a series of plagues to force Pharaoh to let His people go free. He turned the water into blood; He sent frogs and flies; the cattle became sick; and all kinds of terrible things happened. Yet, Pharaoh would not let God's people go free.

God sent one last plague, so terrible that it would force Pharaoh to let His people go. He killed all the firstborn in the land. But He protected all the firstborn of Israel from harm.

Finally, Pharaoh let the people of Israel go free, but soon he changed his mind and followed them with his army. Moses and the people were trapped between Pharaoh's army and the sea.

God had Moses raise his arms over the Red Sea, and it split in two, leaving a path of dry land. All of Israel crossed over the Red Sea on dry land, but when Pharaoh's army was in the middle of the sea, God caused the sea to return to its place and it covered Pharaoh and all of his army.

God feeds His people with manna in the desert.

FORTY YEARS IN THE DESERT

Exodus 15:1—Numbers 14:35

THE people of Israel thanked God for protecting them against the army of Pharaoh at the Red Sea.

God continued to protect them as they traveled through the desert. They ran out of food, so God sent them manna from heaven. Manna looks like a small seed that the people could use to make into bread. Each night the people of Israel collected enough manna for food the next day.

The people became tired of eating only manna, so they began to complain. God sent them many birds, which they could catch and eat.

When the people ran out of water, they began to complain again. God had Moses take his rod and strike a rock, and water came out.

Yet, no matter how many times God gave Israel what they needed, they continued to complain. He even showed them the fruit of the promised land, but they completely refused to trust in God. Finally, the Lord decreed that they would have to dwell in the desert for forty years, until they would learn the ways of the Lord. They would not enter the promised land until all of those who had left Egypt with Moses would have died.

Moses breaks the tablets of the ten commandments.

THE TEN COMMANDMENTS

Exodus 19:1—Deuteronomy 34:12

EVEN though the people of Israel were constantly complaining and doing the things that God had told them not to do, God still loved them. God had Moses remind His people of how He had brought them out of the land of Egypt. He promised them that if they listened to His voice and kept His covenant, they would always be His own special people.

He then gave them a wonderful sign of His love. God had Moses climb up His holy mountain, Mount Sinai. The people were to remain at the base of the mountain while Moses was speaking with the Lord.

God gave Moses the commandments that He wanted His people to follow. These commandments were the way to life, while sin was a choice for death.

The most important commandments were the ten commandments. They are:

1) I am the Lord your God; you shall not have strange gods before Me.
2) You shall not take the name of the Lord, your God, in vain.
3) You shall keep holy the Lord's day.
4) You shall honor your father and your mother.
5) You shall not kill.
6) You shall not commit adultery.
7) You shall not steal.
8) You shall not bear false witness.
9) You shall not covet your neighbor's wife.
10) You shall not covet your neighbor's goods.

Before He went up the mountain, Moses had told his people that they were to stand at the base of the mountain and pray to the Lord.

The people did not obey his instructions, but instead they did what was hateful in the eyes of the Lord. They waited for Moses for a while, but when he still did not return, they decided to make a pagan idol.

They took all of their gold and asked Aaron to melt it and make it into a statue of a bull. When Aaron did as they had told him, they prayed to the golden bull that he had made.

God told Moses what His people were doing, and Moses climbed down the mountain. When he arrived at the camp and saw what the people had done, he dropped the tablets of the commandments and they broke into pieces.

Moses punished the people for the wicked things they had done. He then went back up the mountain, and God once again wrote the ten commandments on two stone tablets.

Moses read the law to the people, and they all promised to follow this law for the rest of their lives.

The people continued to live in the desert until all those who had left Egypt except for Joshua and Caleb were dead (these two men were rewarded for their faith in the Lord).

When Moses had grown very old, he blessed his people and told them to be faithful to God. Then God had him climb to the top of a mountain where God showed him the promised land.

Moses died there and God buried him, for he was a special friend of God.

The walls of Jericho come tumbling down.

ISRAEL ENTERS THE PROMISED LAND

Joshua 1:1—6:27

WHEN Moses died, Joshua became the leader of the people of Israel. He led his people to the Jordan River and he told them to pray so that they might be ready to cross over into the promised land.

Before he crossed the river with all the people, he sent two spies into the land. They went into the city of Jericho to find out how strong the enemy was.

The king of Jericho found out that there were spies from the people of Israel in his city; so he sent troops to arrest them.

In the meantime, the spies arrived at the house of Rahab. She had heard how the Lord was guiding the people of Israel; so she agreed to help the spies if they promised not to harm her family when Israel would conquer the city. This they promised, telling her to tie a scarlet cord to her window so that the men of Israel would know that it was her house and would not harm any of her family.

So Rahab hid the spies on the roof of her house. She told the king's soldiers that they had already left and pointed them in the wrong direction.

The spies found their way back to the people of Israel and told them that the way lay open before them.

Joshua led the people to the river. He had the priests carry the ark to the edge of the river, and the waters parted. They all crossed over on dry land. Joshua built an altar to celebrate the day when the people entered the promised land.

Joshua brought the people to the city of Jericho. The walls of that city were very high and strong, and it seemed almost impossible for the men of Israel to conquer the city. For six days Joshua had the soldiers and the priests go round the city, carrying the ark of the covenant, but they did not make any noise.

Then, on the seventh day, the soldiers and the priests marched around the city as they had the previous six days. This time, though, the priests took their horns and blew them loudly.

The moment that their horns sounded, the walls of the city came tumbling down. The armies of the pagans were completely defeated on that day, for the Lord was with the army of Israel. But the men of Israel were careful not to harm Rahab or any of her family, for she had protected the spies who had gone into Jericho.

The Lord continued to protect the armies of Israel, so they were victorious over all the armies of those who rose up against them.

SAMSON

Judges 13:1—16:31

WHEN the people of Israel entered the promised land, it took them a long time to conquer all of the cities. Most of the people lived in the desert and the mountains for a long time while the pagans continued to live in the fertile areas in the valleys.

God had called His people to follow Him without fear, but every once in a while they would begin to worship the pagan gods. At times like this, God would punish His people by allowing the pagans to be victorious over them.

The people of Israel would realize their mistake and then call upon God for help. Whenever they called upon Him, He would send a hero, a judge, to rescue them from their enemies.

One of the most famous of the judges was Samson. His birth was foretold by an angel who visited his mother and father. The angel told them that their son was to be a nazarite, a person totally dedicated to the Lord. He was never to drink wine or cut his hair.

Samson's parents did just as the angel had commanded, and their son was very powerful. He was able to kill wild beasts with his bare hands. He also defeated many of the enemies of God's people.

One day Samson was visiting a city of the Philistines, the enemies of Israel. There he saw a beautiful woman, Delilah. Samson fell in love with her and married her, but Delilah was an evil woman. She kept trying to find out why Samson was so strong.

At first Samson teased her and did not tell her the truth about the source of his strength, but she finally got him to tell her the true source of his strength: that his hair had never been cut.

The next time Samson fell asleep, she took a razor and shaved his head. When he woke up, he had lost all of his strength. The Philistines were able to throw him in prison where they treated him terribly.

One day the Philistines were celebrating a feast for one of their gods, and they brought Samson out to make fun of him. They tied Samson to two of the main pillars of the temple.

Samson prayed to God and asked Him that he be given his strength just one more time. God answered his prayer and gave him all the strength that he once had. Samson pushed against the pillars of the temple, knocking them down so that the entire building fell down. Samson killed more of the enemies of the Lord on that one day than he had ever killed before.

Samson pulls down the temple of the Philistines.

Boaz sees Ruth collecting grain in the field.

RUTH

Ruth 1:1—4:22

ISRAEL suffered greatly in the days of the judges. People often did not have enough to eat. Naomi and her husband were so poor that they had to take their sons and move from Bethlehem, their home town, to Moab, a pagan land. There Naomi's two sons married women from Moab.

Eventually Naomi's husband died, as did her two sons. She decided to go back to Bethlehem; so she called her two daughters-in-law and and told them to go back to their families. She thought that they could get married again and find some happiness in their lives.

One of these women did as Naomi had said, but Ruth, the other woman, refused to leave Naomi alone. She told Naomi that wherever Naomi would go, she would go. She said, "Your people will be my people, your God will be my God."

So Ruth traveled with Naomi to Bethlehem. When they arrived there, Ruth would go out into the fields to gather loose grain after the workmen so that they would have something to eat. God was very pleased, for Ruth was such a good and generous woman.

One day Ruth was working in the fields of a man named Boaz. When Boaz came out to the fields to inspect the work being done, he noticed Ruth working there. He was moved by her beauty and he asked his foreman who she was. The foreman told him all about her, and Boaz was very impressed for he saw that she was as good as she was beautiful.

Boaz called Ruth over and told her that she could work in his fields any time she wanted. He also instructed his workmen to drop some grain whenever she was working there so that she might take home a good amount.

Ruth told Naomi all about this, and Naomi was very pleased for Boaz was one of their cousins. She told Ruth to go visit him that evening and to sleep by his feet.

When Boaz woke up the next morning and saw Ruth lying there, he decided to marry her. There was only one problem—one man in his family was a closer relative than he and that man had the right to marry Ruth. So he called the man before the elders of the city and asked whether he intended to marry Ruth. The relative answered that he did not; so Boaz was free to marry her.

God blessed Ruth and Boaz and gave them a son whom they named Obed. He would become the grandfather of the great King David.

שְׁמוּאֵל שְׁמוּאֵל

Samuel hears the call of the Lord.

SAMUEL, THE JUDGE AND PROPHET

1 Samuel 1:1—3:8

THE people of Israel continued to turn away from the Lord, so God once again left them in the power of their enemies. When they turned back to the Lord with all their heart, He sent them another leader, the last of the judges, Samuel.

Hannah, the mother of Samuel, was married to a man named Elkanah. One of Elkanah's wives had many children, but Hannah did not yet have any. Elkanah tried to comfort Hannah, but her sorrow was very deep.

Once when they had gone up to the Lord's shrine to worship God, Hannah prayed that Lord would look with favor upon her, His humble servant. She promised that if she had a son, she would dedicate him to the service of the Lord.

The priest Eli was looking on as Hannah was praying. He saw her lips moving, but he did not hear any sound because she was praying in her heart. Eli, however, thought that she was drunk. He began to yell at her for being drunk in the house of the Lord, but she answered that she was not drunk, only praying with all her heart. Eli realized that he had misjudged Hannah, and he sent her on her way, praying that the Lord would grant her request.

Hannah went home and shortly after that she became pregnant. She was overflowing with joy for the Lord had shown her His mercy. When her child was born, she named him Samuel, a name that means God listens, for God had listened to her prayers. She sang a song of joy to celebrate her good fortune and the love of the Lord.

When Samuel had grown old enough to be away from his mother, she took him to the shrine of the Lord to serve the Lord for all of his life.

Some time later Samuel was sleeping in the shrine when he was awakened by a voice that said, "Samuel, Samuel." He went running to Eli and said, "Here I am; why did you call me?" Eli told Samuel that he had not called him and he sent him back to sleep.

A second time Samuel heard his name called and ran to Eli, but again Eli told him that he had not called and he should go back to bed.

Then a third time Samuel heard his name called, and he ran off to Eli. Eli finally realized that it was the Lord who was calling Samuel and he instructed him that if it happened again, he should respond, "Speak, Lord, for your servant is listening."

When Samuel woke up still another time, he answered, "Speak, Lord, for your servant is listening."

From that time on, God spoke to Samuel and revealed many things to him. God made Samuel a priest in place of Eli and his sons, for the sons of Eli were wicked men. Samuel was a good man who was very faithful to the Lord. Whenever the armies of Israel would go out against their enemies, he would pray for them so that the Lord would grant them victory.

Saul is made the king of Israel.

SAUL IS MADE THE KING OF ISRAEL

1 Samuel 3:19—12:25

WHEN Samuel had grown very old, the people visited him to ask him and the Lord for a favor. Up to this time, Israel did not have a king, for God Himself was their king. But the people of Israel wanted to be like all the other nations. So they asked God to give them a king.

Samuel was very angry at this request. After all, God Himself was their king; why would they want a person to take God's place? But the Lord spoke to Samuel and told him to grant their request. So Samuel prayed that the Lord would guide him to choose the right person as king.

Samuel also warned the people that the new king would make life very difficult for them. He would take their sons into his army and their daughters into his court. He would choose the best vineyards and gardens for himself. He would demand that the people give him a tenth of all the grain that they would grow and a tenth of all their flocks.

Yet this did not discourage the people. They continued to insist that Samuel give them a king.

One day a young man from the tribe of Benjamin, Saul, was passing by. Saul's father had sent him to look for some donkeys that were lost. Saul and his companion had traveled far and wide looking for the donkeys, but they had not had any luck in finding them. They decided to stop and visit Samuel, for they thought he might be able to tell them where to look.

As soon as Samuel saw Saul, he knew that he would be the king. Saul was tall and strong, a man who would make a fitting king for Israel.

Samuel had Saul and his friend stay the night, and he greatly honored him at a dinner he had prepared in Saul's honor. Then the next morning he poured the sacred oil over his head, thus making him the king of Israel.

The Spirit of the Lord came upon Saul in a powerful way, and all the people spoke about what had happened to him.

And so the people of Israel made Saul their king. He did all the things about which Samuel had warned them, but the people were pleased for they were now like all the other nations.

Saul led the armies of Israel against all their enemies. At first they were very successful, for Saul did what was pleasing in the eyes of the Lord. God continued to grant them victory as long as Saul was faithful to the Lord.

Samuel tells Saul that God has rejected him.

SAUL IS REJECTED

1 Samuel 13:1—15:35

BUT Saul did not always remain faithful to the ways of the Lord. Once, when the armies of Israel had gathered to do battle against their enemies, Samuel sent Saul a message that he would come and offer a sacrifice in their behalf.

Saul waited a long time for Samuel, an entire week, but Samuel was nowhere to be seen. Saul saw that many of the men in his army were leaving camp and going back to their homes. He feared that, if he waited for Samuel, he might not have enough soldiers to defeat the enemy.

So Saul performed the sacrifice that Samuel had said he would perform.

Just as he was finishing the sacrifice, Samuel arrived. He was very angry because Saul had not waited for him. He told Saul that he had disobeyed the command of the Lord and because of this God would take away his kingdom.

Another time the Lord ordered Saul to burn to the ground a city that his armies had captured. Saul did not do as the Lord had commanded him, and once again Samuel told Saul that God had rejected him and that God would put another man on his throne.

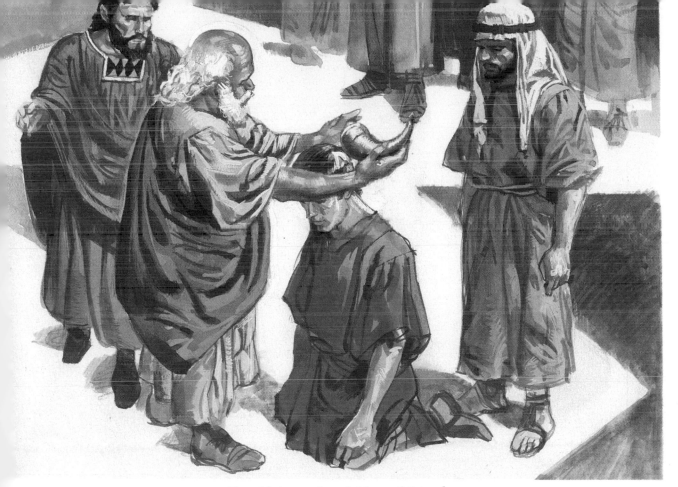

David is anointed king of Israel.

DAVID IS CHOSEN TO BE KING

1 Samuel 16:1-33

SAMUEL knew that the Lord had rejected Saul as king; so he set off to find the one whom God would choose in Saul's place. He traveled to the town of Bethlehem, to the house of a man named Jesse, for the Lord had directed him there.

When he arrived at Jesse's house, he asked to see his sons. Jesse brought his sons out one by one, all handsome and strong men, but Samuel knew that the Lord had not chosen any of them. The Lord did not judge by outward appearances, but by what was in a person's heart.

Finally, Samuel asked Jesse whether he had any other sons. Jesse responded that there was one boy, David, who was out in the fields watching the sheep. Samuel instructed Jesse to send someone for him and to bring him there.

When the boy arrived and was brought before Samuel, the prophet knew that this was the one whom the Lord had called to be king. Although he was the smallest of the sons of Jesse, he had a pure heart that was very pleasing to the Lord. Samuel took the sacred oil and anointed David to be king in the place of Saul.

DAVID AND GOLIATH

1 Samuel 17:1—18:9

ONCE again the enemies of the people of God gathered to attack them. Saul gathered all the soldiers of Israel. But the enemies of Israel had a secret weapon. They had brought a giant with them, Goliath, who challenged all the soldiers of Israel to come out and fight him one on one.

All the soldiers of Israel were very frightened by Goliath. Each day when he would go out into the field and challenge the soldiers of Israel, no one could be found who would go out to fight him. The men of Israel became very discouraged.

David's brothers had gone off to fight with the army of Israel, and Jesse sent his youngest son, David, to bring some extra food to them.

When David arrived at their camp, he heard all about Goliath. He began to ask around why no one was going out to fight him and what reward would be given to the one who would do battle with Goliath.

Eventually word of this reached Saul who called for the boy. Saul told David that he was too young to fight against Goliath, but David answered that he could defeat him.

David said that he had often fought with bears and lions while guarding his father's sheep and had always defeated them. Surely the Lord would lead him to victory over this Philistine.

So Saul sent David out to fight Goliath. He clothed him in his armor and gave him his sword, but they were too big for him to carry. David took off the armor and put down the sword. He gathered five smooth stones and put them in his bag. Then he took his slingshot and went out to fight Goliath.

When Goliath saw David approaching, he insulted him and laughed out loud, for David appeared to be so small. He asked David whether he was a dog for David to have come out after him with a stick.

But David took a stone out and put it in his sling. He hurled it and it struck Goliath on his forehead. It knocked Goliath out, and David ran over to him and took Goliath's own sword and cut off his head.

David became a great hero in Israel because of this. The women would sing that Saul was victorious over thousands and David was victorious over tens of thousands. He became so famous and so popular that Saul became very jealous of him. Saul knew that the Lord had rejected him and that the Lord loved David in a special way, and he could not bear it. He became so insane with jealousy that he even tried to kill David.

David defeats Goliath with his sling.

David dances before the ark of the covenant.

DAVID BECOMES THE KING OF ISRAEL

1 Samuel 18:1—2 Samuel 7:29

AS time went on, it became more and more obvious that the Lord had chosen David. Whenever Saul went out to battle, he would be defeated while David would be victorious. Finally, Saul and two of his sons were killed in battle against the enemies of Israel.

The two tribes of the south made David their king, while the ten tribes of the north decided to crown one of the sons of Saul as their king.

This lasted for seven years and six months until the son of Saul was killed by two of his enemies. David punished these men, for they had dared to harm an anointed one of the Lord.

The tribes of the north came to visit David and asked him to become king over all Israel. He ruled over all of Israel for thirty-three years.

One of the first things that David did when he became king was to capture the city of Jerusalem. Until then it had been a city ruled by the pagans. Now, David took it from them and made it the capital of his kingdom.

David decided that Jerusalem should also be the center of the Jewish faith. Up until then, the ark of the covenant, the holiest thing that the Jews possessed, was kept in a shrine and, at times, it was moved from place to place.

Now David decided that it should be brought into Jerusalem so that all the Jewish people would visit the city when they wanted to pray to their God.

So David and the priests and many of the people went down and brought the ark into the city of Jerusalem. They performed many sacrifices along the way, and David danced before the ark to give glory to God. From that time on, Jerusalem would be the holy city of the Lord.

After a while, David realized that something was wrong. He had built a magnificent palace for himself but the ark of the covenant was still housed in a tent. He visited the prophet Nathan and asked him whether he should build a temple to the Lord.

Nathan prayed to the Lord and received the answer that he was to give to David. Nathan told David that he was not to build a house for the Lord, for God was the one who was going to build a house for him. He was going to give David descendants who would sit upon his throne forever.

One day one of his descendants, Jesus, would fulfill what had been promised to David.

DAVID AND ABSALOM

1 Samuel 11:1—19:10

NOT everything that David did was good. At times, he sinned and turned away from the Lord.

Once, while he was walking on the roof of the palace, he noticed a woman on the roof of a neighboring building. She was very beautiful, and he invited her over to the palace. Her name was Bathsheba, and she was a married woman, but that did not stop David from sinning with her.

Bathsheba became pregnant and she told David; so he called her husband home from the war. David was hoping that her husband would go home and sleep with his wife and therefore think that the child was his.

But Bathsheba's husband refused to go home, for that was not allowed during times of war. When David realized that he would not go home, he arranged with the general in charge of the war to have Bathsheba's husband killed in battle.

Some time later Nathan the prophet came to the palace and asked David to judge a case. Nathan spoke of a man who had only one small sheep that he loved; it was almost part of his family. This man had a rich neighbor who had many sheep, but when the rich man received a visitor, he killed the poor man's sheep for his dinner.

David was furious and said that this man should be punished.

Nathan then turned to David and told him that he was that man, for he had sinned against the husband of Bathsheba. Now God would punish him for what he had done.

One of the punishments David received was that he had much sadness caused by the members of his own family.

David's son, Absalom, rebelled against him and chased him out of Jerusalem. David truly loved Absalom, and this rebellion hurt him deeply.

David sent his general to fight against Absalom and his army. Absalom's troops were defeated, and Absalom fled for his life.

David had given very strict orders to capture Absalom, for he did not want his son to be killed.

As Absalom was fleeing, his hair got caught in the low branches of a tree. He was left hanging between heaven and earth. When David's troops came upon him, they put him to death, in spite of David's order.

The messengers ran from the field to tell David that his army had won the battle. David asked the messengers if his son was safe, but one of the messengers told him that Absalom had been killed.

David was deeply troubled when he heard this, and he wept for many days.

Absalom is caught in the tree by his hair.

Solomon shows his great wisdom in judging between two women.

KING SOLOMON

1 Kings 1:1—3:28

WHEN David was quite old, Bathsheba came to visit him. She asked him who the next king of Israel would be. She told him that he had promised to make their son, Solomon, the next king. Bathsheba also told David that one of his other sons was already claiming to be king, even though David was still alive.

David was enraged when he heard that his son was trying to take his crown. He called Solomon to the palace and had him crowned as king at once. Thus, when David would die, everyone would know that Solomon was to be the next king.

Solomon realized that it was very difficult to be a good king and he was still very young. He was not sure that he could do a good job. He visited a shrine of the Lord and asked God to give him the gift of wisdom so that he could govern God's people well. God was very pleased to hear this request. He told Solomon that because he had asked for wisdom and not for riches or glory, he would receive his request.

Of all the kings of Israel, Solomon was truly the wisest. One day two women appeared before him bringing a very confusing case for judgment.

The first woman told Solomon that she lived in the same house as the other woman. She had given birth to a child, and the other woman also had a child three days later. During the night, the baby of the other woman had died. She told Solomon that the other woman had gotten up in the middle of the night and switched her dead baby for the first woman's live child. When the first woman awoke in the morning, she found the dead child. But when she examined it, she realized that it was not her baby—it was the other woman's child.

When it came time for the second woman to talk, she denied everything that the first woman had said. She said that it was the first woman's child who had died and that the baby which was still alive was hers.

How would Solomon decide which of these women was the mother of the child that was still alive? After he considered the matter and prayed for a little while, he ordered that the baby be cut in two and half of it be given to each of the mothers.

The woman who had lied said that she thought this was a fair solution, but the true mother of the baby cried out and said that she preferred that the baby stay alive and be given to the other mother. Thus, Solomon knew who the true mother was, the one who loved the baby so much that she would give him up rather than see him die.

Solomon builds a great temple in Jerusalem.

SOLOMON BUILDS THE TEMPLE

1 Kings 5:1—10:29

SOLOMON was so filled with wisdom that he became famous all over the world. People would come from Egypt and from the East just to see him and to listen to what he said.

He was also famous for the many buildings that he built. He built a beautiful palace and cities to house his army. But the most famous building that he built was the temple of the Lord in Jerusalem. His father David had asked the prophet Nathan if he could build a house for the Lord, but God had told David that he would not build Him a house, but rather God would build a house for him. It was also said that God did not allow David to build a temple because he had shed too much blood during his life.

Now, however, the Lord blessed Solomon's plan. The first thing that Solomon did was to make a treaty with King Hiram of Tyre to help him build the temple. In return, Solomon would provide much food for Hiram's kingdom. Hiram was very pleased with this agreement, and his workmen and men sent by Solomon set to work to provide all the wood needed for the temple.

In the meantime, Solomon sent other workmen to cut huge blocks of stone out of the earth. Because these stones were going to be used in the temple, Solomon decreed that they had to be cut without any tools made from metal.

The temple was going to be about ninety feet long, thirty feet wide, and forty feet high. Its walls were made of stone that was covered by cedar wood on the outside. Its roof was made of wood.

In the center of the temple was a special room called the Holy of Holies. It was thirty feet long, thirty feet wide, and thirty feet high. This was where the ark of the covenant was kept.

The builders used much gold in the temple. The inside of the temple, the altar, and the angels made of wood were all covered with gold.

In all, it took Solomon seven years to build the temple. He also had many beautiful objects made to decorate the temple.

Solomon built a golden altar, a golden table upon which the holy bread was placed, lampstands of pure gold, and many other things. Everything was very beautiful.

God was very pleased with the temple that Solomon had built. The priests carried the ark of the covenant into the Holy of Holies, and when they left that holy place, they saw that a cloud had filled it. When Solomon saw the cloud, he knew that God would dwell in this temple.

Solomon knew that the heavens and the earth were not large enough to contain the presence of God, and yet God would lower Himself to make Himself present in a special way in this temple. He and all the people of Israel greatly rejoiced.

When the people would fall into sin from then on, they knew there was a place where they could go to ask for the mercy of God. They also knew that God had made a promise to them to be present whenever they would call upon Him in faith.

People from all over the world came to see the beautiful temple that Solomon had built for the God of Israel. They were filled with wonder, for it was the most beautiful building that they had ever seen.

Solomon builds temples to pagan gods.

SOLOMON SINS

1 Kings 11:1—43

SOLOMON was married many, many times. In fact, he had one thousand wives. Many of these wives were from pagan lands, and they tempted Solomon to sin and turn away from the ways of the Lord.

These wives asked Solomon whether they might worship their own gods in Israel. Solomon not only let them worship their false gods, he even built temples for the pagan gods.

Then, to make things even worse, the foreign wives invited Solomon to pray to their gods and to offer sacrifices to them. Solomon began to do this, greatly offending the Lord.

Because of this sin, the Lord allowed the enemies of Israel to rebel against Israel and to gain their independence.

Therefore, the kingdom of Israel could no longer enjoy the peace that it had seen during the early days of Solomon's reign.

The worst punishment that God visited upon Solomon and the kingdom of Israel was that He decreed that after Solomon died, the kingdom would be divided.

The prophet speaks of the division of the kingdom.

THE KINGDOM IS DIVIDED

1 Kings 11:26—12:20

ONE day a prophet of the Lord met a man named Jeroboam. The prophet took off his robe and tore it into twelve pieces. He gave ten pieces to Jeroboam and told him that God would divide the tribes of Israel and ten of them would be under his reign. Only two would be ruled by the son of Solomon.

When Solomon died, his son Rehoboam became the king of Israel. All of the leaders of Israel visited Rehoboam and told him that things had been very difficult under his father, Solomon. It had cost them much to build the temple, the palace, and the cities that Solomon had built. They asked Rehoboam if he would be a gentler king than his father. The king asked the advice of the elders, and they all told him to listen to the people.

But Rehoboam was foolish. He told the people that he would make them pay even more and he would treat them more harshly.

And so the ten tribes of the north broke away from Jerusalem and formed a new kingdom under Jeroboam who would be their king.

Elijah prays before his sacrifice on Mount Carmel.

ELIJAH THE PROPHET

1 Kings 17:1—21:29

ONE of the kings of Israel married a princess named Jezebel who came from a pagan land. She was a very wicked woman, and she convinced the king to punish those who worshiped the Lord.

At this time, there was a great prophet of the Lord named Elijah. He proclaimed that there would be a great drought in the land, and it did not rain for three years. This was a punishment to show the people that it was the Lord who gave the rain and not Baal.

During the drought, Elijah traveled to the north. He came across a widow and asked her for something to eat. She told him that she only had enough flour and oil for one meal for herself and her son. But Elijah told her to do as he said. She obeyed and she had enough food not only for that day but for the rest of the drought.

Elijah challenged the priests of Baal to a contest to find out whether Baal or the Lord was the only true God. They gathered on top of Mount Carmel and both prepared sacrifices to their god.

The priests of Baal prayed to Baal, asking him to send fire from the heavens. But there was no answer. So they began to dance and sing and even cut themselves, but there still was no answer. Elijah mocked them and told them to yell louder because maybe their god was asleep. But no matter what they did, they never received an answer, for their god was a false god.

When the priests of Baal were too tired to continue, Elijah took his turn. He ordered that water be poured over the sacrifice so that it would be very wet. Elijah then called upon the Lord. He prayed that God send His fire upon the offering so that everyone could see that He was the only true God.

As soon as Elijah finished praying, God sent His fire down upon the sacrifice and completely burned it up, even though it had been very wet. All the people confessed that they had done what was wrong when they had worshiped Baal. They asked God for forgiveness for their many sins.

Because the people of Israel had turned back to God, He ended that drought that He had sent upon the land. But even then Jezebel continued to do evil things.

There was a certain man named Naboth who owned a vineyard near the king's palace. He refused to sell it to the king. Jezebel arranged for Naboth to be accused of doing terrible things. He was placed on trial and put to death. Then she gave the land to her husband, the king.

Elijah heard about all the things that Jezebel had done. He visited the king and told him that he and Jezebel would be punished by the Lord, for they had caused the death of an innocent man, and they had greatly offended the Lord.

— 65 —

Elisha parts the water with Elijah's cloak.

ELISHA

2 Kings 2:1—5:1

ONE day Elijah went up the mountain of the Lord. He prayed inside a cave upon the mountain and then went out to meet the Lord.

At first, Elijah heard a strong wind upon the mountain, but the Lord was not in the wind. Then there was an earthquake, but the Lord was not in the earthquake. After the earthquake there was fire upon the mountain, but the Lord was not in the fire. Finally, there was a quiet, gentle breeze upon the mountain, and the Lord was in that breeze.

The message from this revelation was that the Lord speaks not only in great and powerful ways but also in normal everyday events.

When Elijah came down the mountain, he saw a man named Elisha plowing his field. Elijah took off his cloak and threw it over him. Elisha realized that this meant that he was being called to follow Elijah and to be a prophet of the Lord.

When it came time for Elijah to be called home by the Lord, he went into the desert with Elisha. Elijah told Elisha to ask for whatever he desired.

Elisha asked Elijah for a double portion of his spirit. Elijah answered that if Elisha would see him taken up into the heavens, then he would receive his wish.

As they walked on, a great flaming chariot descended from the heavens and Elijah was taken up into the heavens.

Elisha was a great prophet in the land for he had received a double portion of Elijah's spirit. He performed many miracles in the name of the Lord.

Once he helped a widow of one of the prophets of the Lord. She owned only one jar of oil and owed much money.

Elisha told her to borrow many pots and pour oil from the jar into the pots. The oil was multiplied so much that the widow could pay all her debts.

The most famous miracle that Elisha performed was the cure of Naaman the Syrian. Naaman was a pagan and he was stricken by leprosy. He visited the man of God and asked him to cure him.

Elisha sent word to Naaman that he should wash in the Jordan River seven times and he would be cured. At first Naaman refused to do this, for he had expected the prophet to perform some miraculous action and he resented the fact that Elisha had told him to do such a simple thing.

But when Naaman finally did as the prophet had commanded, he was totally cured of his leprosy.

God cleanses the lips of Isaiah, the prophet.

ISAIAH, THE PROPHET OF HOLINESS

The Book of the Prophet Isaiah

GOD continued to send His holy prophets to the people of Israel to call them back to His ways. This time he called Isaiah, a prophet from the southern kingdom of Judah.

One day Isaiah was praying in the temple when he saw a vision of the throne of the Lord. It was surrounded by seraphs, angels with six wings.

They sang the praises of the Lord without ceasing. They sang, "Holy, holy, holy is the Lord of hosts. All the earth is filled with His glory."

Isaiah was afraid, for he realized that he was a sinner living in a nation of sinners. One of the angels took a burning coal from the altar and touched it to Isaiah's lips, thus making them holy and worthy of speaking the Word of the Lord.

The prophet went out and spoke to the king. These were very dangerous times, for the kings of Israel and Syria were sending their armies against Jerusalem. The king of Jerusalem wanted to send a message to the king of Assyria to ask for his help.

Isaiah told him that he should not do this, for he should trust in the Lord. God would deliver him from all his enemies.

Isaiah then told the king that he should ask for a sign from the Lord as proof that the Lord would indeed protect him. But the king told Isaiah that he would not ask for a sign.

The king wanted to continue trusting in the power of a pagan king. He did not want to trust in the Lord.

Isaiah told the king that God would send him a sign even if he did not ask for one. Isaiah told the king that a young maiden would bear a child who would be named Emmanuel.

This child would be the prince of peace who would bring peace to God's land. The peace would be so great that the wolf would lie down with the lamb, the calf with the lion. There would be no harm or ruin on all of God's holy mountain.

Later in the book of the prophet we see other promises made to the people of Israel. They had suffered greatly at the hands of their enemies. God called out to His people and promised them that He would console them. He would once again fill their hearts with joy.

Jerusalem would once again be God's holy city. People from all over the world would come to bring gifts to the Lord and to His holy people.

The people of the north are led away into exile.

THE EXILE OF THE NORTH

1 Kings 17:1—19, 37; The Books of the Prophets Amos and Hosea

THE people of the north continued to turn away from the Lord. The Lord sent prophets to call them back to His ways, but the people just would not listen to them. They continued to follow the evil ways that Jezebel had taught them.

The Lord sent the prophet Amos to preach to the people of Israel. He told the people that God would punish them. He pointed out that God had shown them His love, but instead of remaining faithful to His ways, they had wandered far from the ways of the Lord.

Amos condemned the rich people of the land for the terrible way that they were treating the poor people. They cheated them and stole from them the few things that they owned. They even stole the bread from their children's mouths.

Because of this, God would defend the children of the poor and punish those who had stolen their food.

The Lord also sent the prophet Hosea to preach to the people. Hosea spoke of how much the Lord loved Israel and how God's covenant with Israel was like a marriage between a husband and a wife. But Israel had betrayed the Lord and had worshiped the pagan gods.

Again, the prophet told Israel that it would be punished for betraying the Lord.

Both Amos and Hosea also spoke of the day when the Lord would finish the days of punishment and would again show His mercy to the people of Israel.

Even after all these warnings, Israel did not turn back to the Lord. In fact, the king of Israel did something that was worse than anything the people of Israel had ever done before. He made a treaty with the king of Syria, a pagan nation, to attack the king and the people of Jerusalem. He would be helping a pagan defeat the people of the Lord.

And so the Lord punished the king and the people of the north. He had the king of Assyria send his armies up against the cities of Israel. They destroyed every town and city. They stole all the gold and silver from the shrines and palaces.

The invaders also took all the leading people of the land as prisoners. They led them away from their cities and their land. But they did not take the poor people away; they let them stay in Israel.

The soldiers of Assyria led the rich people off to the land of Assyria where they would be slaves and servants of the people who dwelt there. Then the Assyrians rebuilt all the cities and towns that they had destroyed and they moved a new people there, a people who did not know the Lord.

The sons and the daughters of this pagan people married the sons and the daughters of the poor people of Israel.

The people who remained in the land began to pray to God in a strange way, for they now prayed like the pagans who were living in their land. When the people of the south heard this, they warned the people of the north that this was wrong. They told them that they should not allow their sons and their daughters to marry pagans, but the people of the north did not listen.

Soon the people of the north, the people of God and the pagans, became a new people. From then on they were called the Samaritans.

Jeremiah proclaims God's judgment upon the people.

JEREMIAH, A PROPHET TO THE NATIONS

The Book of the Prophet Jeremiah

WHEN the people of Judah saw what had happened to the kingdom of the north, they should have learned the lesson and should have returned to the Lord. But even then the people turned away from God. They worshiped pagan gods and continued to rob the food of the poor.

So God sent another prophet, a powerful messenger of the Word of the Lord. This prophet was Jeremiah. He was to be a prophet to the nations.

Jeremiah was called by the Lord at a very young age. At first he was afraid to speak the words of the Lord. He thought that no one would pay any attention to him because he was so young. But the Lord answered him that he had been chosen to be a prophet of the Lord even before he was born. The Lord would protect him from all his enemies.

So Jeremiah was a fearless messenger of the Word of the Lord. He never got married as a warning to Israel that the time was short: that they could not waste time. But they would not listen to the message of the Lord. Jeremiah told the king to surrender to his enemies and to trust in God's care, but he would not trust in the Lord.

The people of Jerusalem are led away into exile.

JERUSALEM IS DESTROYED

2 Kings 24:1—25:30

THE army of Judah continued to fight against their enemies, the army of Babylon, until they were totally defeated.

The king of Babylon punished the people of Jerusalem for not surrendering to his army. He burned the entire city. He even destroyed the temple, the place where God spoke to His people. He stole all the holy things that were kept in the temple, and everything else that could be carried away.

All the important people in the land were taken away into exile. The soldiers dragged away the king and his wife, the princes, the priests, and the prophets.

The people who were carried away suffered terribly. For a long time there was not enough food or clothing. They became servants and slaves in a foreign land.

Worst of all, the people did not know if the Lord would listen to their prayers anymore.

They knew that they deserved this punishment for all the evil things they had done, but now they wanted to turn back to the Lord.

In a vision, Ezekiel sees the glory of the Lord.

EZEKIEL AND THE PROMISE OF A RETURN

The Book of the Prophet Ezekiel

THE Prophet Ezekiel had a vision of the Lord and began preaching just before Jerusalem was destroyed. He tried to warn the people with words and deeds to turn back to the Lord.

Once Ezekiel shaved off his beard. He burned a third of it; he took another third and hit it with his sword; and the final third he threw to the wind. This was a sign that the city would be burned and the people would be scattered to the wind.

Another time Ezekiel put on poor clothes and carried all he owned with him, as someone would do if he were going into exile. The people understood that it meant that they would be defeated and carried away into exile.

Finally, God told Ezekiel that his wife was going to die, but Ezekiel was not to mourn for her. The people asked him why he did not cry for his wife, and he answered that the judgment of the Lord was coming upon His city and His people. All would be destroyed and many would die. There would be no time to mourn because they would all be carried away.

The people of Jerusalem would not listen to any of these warnings. They refused to turn back to the Lord, so God sent His punishment upon them. He allowed the king of Babylon to conquer His people. His holy city Jerusalem was burned to the ground. God's people were taken into exile.

Soon they called out to the Lord and asked for His forgiveness. So God gave Ezekiel a new message, one of consolation. Ezekiel told the people that the holy city of Jerusalem would be rebuilt. The temple of the Lord, the place where God spoke to His people, would be more beautiful than it had ever been before. And more important, God would give a new heart to His people. God would remove their hearts of stone and give them hearts filled with love.

The prophet had a vision in which he saw a field with dry bones. God told Ezekiel to preach to these bones. When he did this, the bones were filled with God's own breath, and they took on flesh once more and became a mighty people. This was God's promise that even though His people seemed to be dead, He would give them a share in His own life.

Another time Ezekiel had a vision in which he saw a stream of water flowing out of the temple. At first the stream was shallow, but it became so deep that one could not walk through it. It flowed out into the desert lands and made them fertile. Ezekiel realized that this, too, was a promise from God. This vision meant that when God's people would pray in the temple, they would receive a special gift of grace from the Lord. This gift would give life to God's people, a life that would never end.

THE SUFFERING OF JOB

The Book of Job

THE years of exile were very difficult for the people of God, and they began to wonder about their pain and suffering. They could understand why God would punish those who had sinned, but what about all those who were innocent and were still suffering?

Around that time, they told the story of a man named Job. He was very rich, having many children and many possessions. He always thanked the Lord for the many good things that he had received.

One day Satan spoke to the Lord about Job. He told God that Job only prayed to Him because of the many good things that God had given him. He said that if God would take them back, Job would no longer pray to Him.

So God allowed Satan to take away from Job all the good things the Lord had given him. Satan killed Job's children and destroyed all his animals, his house, and everything that he owned. Job was left sick and alone on a pile of ashes.

Still Job would not curse the Lord. He prayed:

The Lord gave and the Lord has
   taken away;
   blessed be the name of the Lord.
We accept good things from God;
   and should we not accept evil?

Even Job's wife told him that he should get it over with; she told him to curse God and die. But Job still refused to curse the Lord.

Three of Job's friends came to visit and comfort him. Almost immediately they began to accuse him.

The friends said that God would not allow Job to suffer if he had not sinned. They told him to confess his sins and God would take away his punishment.

But Job knew that he had done nothing wrong. He refused to say that he had sinned, for he had not. He asked only that the Lord appear to him and explain why he was suffering.

The Lord appeared to Job and spoke to him. He asked Job if he knew where the snows were stored during the summer. God asked Job if he had created the stars.

God continued to ask Job all kinds of questions, but Job did not know the answers to any of God's questions.

So Job turned to the Lord and admitted that God was more powerful and wise than he. Job said he would trust in God, even if he was suffering.

God was very pleased with Job. He told Job that he was right and Job's friends were very wrong. He returned to Job even more than he had lost, for Job trusted God even in times of pain.

Job tries to trust in the Lord throughout his sufferings.

The people return home from their exile.

THE EXILE ENDS

Isaiah 40:1—66:24; Ezekiel 1:1—10:44; Haggai 1:1—2:23

THROUGH all these difficulties, God continued to listen to His people. He sent many prophets to renew the promises that He had made to them.

These prophets promised that God would once again comfort His people. He would lead His people back to the land of Israel. There He would once again bless them. They would worship Him in His temple, and all would know that He was their God and they were His people.

God said through the prophet Isaiah:

All you who are thirsty,
    come to the water!
You who have no money,
    come, receive grain and eat;
Come, without paying and without
        cost,
    drink wine and milk!
Why spend your money for what is
        not bread;
    your wages for what fails to
        satisfy?

These and many other words brought joy to the people of Israel. Then the Lord fulfilled His promises.

The king of Babylon was filled with pride. He believed that he could do anything he wanted. But the Lord was more powerful than he. The Lord sent Cyrus, the leader of the Persians, who attacked Babylon and defeated its king.

Cyrus became the leader of all these lands. He was a pagan, yet he was a good man who did what the Lord wanted. Cyrus decided to send all those people who were in exile back to the land of their birth. He gave each of these nations money to rebuild their cities and the temples to their gods.

The people of Israel could not believe their good fortune. Word went through all the towns of that land that any Jew who wished to return to Israel was free to go.

As the time drew closer for them to leave, many of the Jews decided not to go back. The first Jews to return would have to build new cities, plant new fields, and work very hard. It was safer for them to stay there rather than to go to Israel.

Some of the Jews found the courage to make this long journey. Those who did not go collected much food and money and gave it to those who were going back. They prayed for them and asked God to protect them.

When the Jews arrived in Israel, it was even worse than they had feared. Everything had been destroyed. All was in ruin. The people who returned were busy trying to grow food and build homes for themselves. Even though they had promised to rebuild the temple of the Lord, they did not keep their promise for a long, long time.

The Lord sent prophets to remind the Jews of their promise. He sent Haggai to tell them that the Lord would send His blessings upon them if they would rebuild the temple.

The Jews listened to Haggai and began to build the temple, but they soon became disappointed for they were too poor to build it as it had been built before. Haggai told them not to be discouraged, for God would make the temple more beautiful than it ever was before.

The Samaritans came up to Jerusalem and asked whether they could help rebuild the temple and the wall of the city. The Jews refused to let them help for they had married the pagans. From then on the Jews and the Samaritans were most bitter enemies.

Nehemiah directs the task of rebuilding the walls of Jerusalem.

NEHEMIAH REBUILDS JERUSALEM

The Book of Nehemiah

MANY years after the Jews had returned, they still had not completed rebuilding their city.

One of the very important officials in the court of the king of Persia was a Jewish man named Nehemiah. He heard reports that conditions in Jerusalem were very difficult. He decided that he had to work to make things better.

Nehemiah asked the king if it would be possible for him to go back to the land of his ancestors. The king gave him letters to present to the governors of that place. They were to allow Nehemiah to do whatever was necessary.

One of the first things Nehemiah did was to speak to the rich people of the land. They had been buying the children of the poor as slaves.

Nehemiah told them that this was not the way of the Lord. He told them that they should help those people out of love for the Lord.

Nehemiah also began to rebuild the walls of Jerusalem. This was the most important work to finish for it would protect the people against the attacks of their enemies. There were some men who tried to stop Nehemiah from completing this project, but they could not do so for the Lord was with Nehemiah.

Ezra proclaims the law to the people of Israel.

EZRA AND THE LAW

The Book of Ezra

THE Jews also had to address their life of faith. They did not keep the law of the Lord for many of them had never learned it.

So Ezra called all the people together. He read the entire book of the law of the Lord and explained its meaning to them. The people began to weep, for they realized that they had been sinning, but Ezra told them not to weep. He told them that this was a day of joy, which they should celebrate, for this was a new beginning.

Ezra was very clear that the sons of Israel were no longer to marry the daughters of the pagans. This was the sin that the Samaritans had committed. From then on they were to marry only men and women from the people of the Lord.

The people were also told that they were to keep the Sabbath holy. They should have nothing to do with those who sold them goods on the Sabbath, for it was to be a day of rest.

The people promised Ezra and the Lord that from then on they would keep the laws of the Lord.

JONAH AND THE WHALE

The Book of Jonah

THE Israelites knew God loved Israel, but they thought that He hated the pagan nations. But how could God hate them, for He had created them? To answer this question, they told the story of the prophet Jonah.

God spoke to Jonah one day and told him to go to the city of Nineveh. He was to proclaim that God was going to punish their city for the people's many sins. Jonah was very disturbed. He hated the people of Nineveh and he did not want to preach to them for they might convert and not be punished by the Lord. He wanted them to be punished.

So Jonah fled and got on a ship going to a distant land. A powerful storm broke out and soon the ship was in danger of sinking. The sailors asked who was at fault for this terrible punishment. They drew lots and discovered that it was Jonah's fault. Jonah admitted that he was running away from the Lord, and he told them to throw him overboard so that they would not die. They did this, and a large fish swallowed Jonah. He remained safe in the belly of the fish for three days, and then the fish spit him up on the shore.

Jonah realized that he could no longer run away from the Lord so he set off for Nineveh. He proclaimed that it would be destroyed on account of its sins. Nineveh was a large city, and it took three days to go from one end to the other. Jonah had gone a single day's journey when the king heard about Jonah's message. He declared that all the people of Nineveh must turn to the Lord and ask for mercy. He proclaimed a fast for all the people and all the animals. The Lord was very pleased with all that the king had ordered. He decided that Nineveh would no longer be punished, for they had converted and prayed to Him.

Jonah was very angry that the Lord had turned back His punishment from Nineveh. He believed that because they were pagans, they did not deserve the mercy of the Lord. So he traveled outside the city and sat alone. The Lord caused a vine to grow over his head. Jonah was pleased with this, for it was hot, and the vine gave him shade. That night God sent a worm into the vine. The worm ate the stem of the vine and it died. The next morning Jonah saw that the vine was dead and he was very disturbed.

The Lord spoke to Jonah and asked him how this was possible. He was disturbed that a vine would die, but he did not care about the people of Nineveh. There were one hundred and twenty thousand people in that city, people whom the Lord had created and loved. Were they not more important than a plant?

This story taught an important lesson to the people of Israel. God loves all people, no matter what their country or language or religion might be. If God loves them, then so should we.

Jonah is freed from the belly of the whale.

Esther is crowned the queen of the Persians.

QUEEN ESTHER

The Book of Esther

THE Jews often had to suffer for their faith. One example of this is a courageous woman who lived during the years when the Persians ruled over Israel.

In the beginning of her story, we hear about a Jewish man named Mordecai. He discovered that some of the king's officials were plotting against the king. Mordecai informed the king about this plot, so the king rewarded him by making him one of the officials at his court. Now there was an evil man at court, Haman, who was jealous of Mordecai and hated him and the Jewish people.

Soon afterward, the king became angry at his queen. He removed her as queen and made it known that he was looking for a new wife who would become the next queen.

Mordecai was the foster-father of a beautiful young woman named Esther.

When the king sent out word to bring all the beautiful women to his court, she was brought in before him. He immediately fell in love with her and made Esther his new queen.

Around this time, Mordecai greatly angered Haman. All the servants at the palace were accustomed to bowing down whenever Haman passed by, but Mordecai refused to bow down (for he only paid honor to God).

Haman hated Mordecai for this, and when he found out that Mordecai was a Jew, he decided to get even by punishing the entire Jewish people.

Haman convinced the king that the Jewish people were very evil and that they should all be punished. The king sent out letters to all the provinces saying that on a certain day all the Jews in the land were to be put to death.

Mordecai heard about this order and went off to see Esther. He told her that she must beg the king for mercy, for she was the only one who could save her people.

At first Esther did not want to help, for she believed that it would be too dangerous for her. There was a law that no one could come before the king unless he invited that person. Yet Mordecai insisted that she had to do something.

Esther then turned to the Lord for help. She fasted and prayed for a long time, telling the Lord that she was placing all her hope in Him. She then dressed up in her best clothes, and she was more beautiful than she had ever been before.

When she arrived at the palace, the king invited her in and promised her anything that she wanted. All she asked for that day was to invite him to a dinner she had prepared.

At that dinner, she invited the king and Haman to still another meal. While they were eating, she told the king that Haman planned to harm a great hero of the king, Mordecai.

The king was so disturbed when he heard this that he went outside to think. While he was outside, Haman fell at the feet of Esther to ask for mercy.

When the king reentered, he was greatly upset, for he saw Haman at Esther's feet and thought that Haman was trying to be her lover. The king decreed that Haman was to be punished.

The king hanged Haman with the very rope that he had planned to use on Mordecai. He also sent letters all over the kingdom that the Jews were not to be harmed by anyone.

Jews still celebrate the feast of Purim to remember the fact that the Lord had delivered them from their enemies through the hands of Esther.

Daniel interprets the sacred writing on the wall.

DANIEL AND THE WRITING
ON THE WALL

Daniel 5:1—31

ANOTHER of the heroes about whom the Jewish people told stories was the prophet Daniel. Although Daniel had lived many years before, his stories became very popular when the Jewish people were being persecuted for their faith. For he had risked his life to be faithful to the end.

A very popular story concerned some writing upon the wall. It took place in the palace of the king of Babylon. The king was throwing a party and wanted to impress the people whom he had invited. He ordered his servants to bring bring all the gold and silver cups and dishes that had been taken out of the temple in Jerusalem. They put wine in the cups and drank from them, all the while praising the power of their own pagan gods.

Suddenly, everyone who was there at the party saw the fingers of a hand. It was writing something on the wall. The king was filled with fear, but no one who was there could understand what had been written upon the wall.

The king called all the wise men to his palace so that they could read and interpret the writing upon the wall. When they arrived, they all looked at what had been written, but not one of them could understand what it meant.

The queen heard what had happened and went over to speak to the king. She told him that she knew of a man who could help him find out what the writing meant.

The queen said that the king's father had brought a great wise man from the land of the Jews. This man, Daniel, was filled with the Spirit of the Lord. He was able to interpret many dreams and solve many difficult problems.

The king's father had been so impressed with him that he had made him the leader of the king's wise men.

So Daniel was brought in, and the king spoke with him. The king explained what had happened and how no one could understand what it meant. The king offered him great rewards if he could explain the writing to him.

Daniel answered the king and told him that he did not want his gifts. He would explain the meaning of the writing to him.

Daniel told the king that the Lord had given his father a great kingdom, but his father had allowed his heart to be filled with pride. The Lord had punished him until he realized that it was the Lord who had all power and until he learned humility.

Now the Lord was ready to punish the king as he had punished his father. The king had allowed himself to do terrible things for he had used the holy cups from the temple for his party.

Daniel told the king that the words written upon the wall were *Mane*, *Thecel*, and *Phares*.

Mane meant that God had decided to put an end to his kingdom. *Thecel* meant that God had weighed him upon a scale and had found him wanting. *Phares* meant that his kingdom would be divided between two other peoples.

That very night the Lord fulfilled what had been written. The king of the Persians and the Medes conquered the entire land.

When the Jews heard this story, they realized that they did not have to fear the king of Syrians, who was persecuting them. For God would overthrow him as quickly as he had overthrown the king of Babylon.

Daniel is thrown into the lions' den.

DANIEL AND THE LIONS' DEN

Daniel 6:1-28

ANOTHER story that the Jews told about Daniel spoke of his great courage in giving witness to the ways of the Lord.

According to this story, Darius, the king of the Medes, had divided his kingdom into many provinces. He placed three men in charge of all the governors, one of whom was Daniel the prophet.

Daniel was a good and honest man and he was an excellent official of the king. The other officials were very jealous of him and plotted to get him into trouble.

All the governors visited the king and praised him for his greatness. They told him that he should make a special law. For thirty days, no one was to give honor to any god or any man except for the king. If someone did bow down to another, he was to be thrown into a den of lions.

The king was very pleased with this idea and made this the law.

Even though Daniel had heard about this law, he continued to go to his house three times a day to pray to the Lord. He would go to his upper room and open the window facing Jerusalem and kneel down, saying his prayers out loud.

The other governors knew what he was doing; they rushed in and caught him while he was kneeling down to God.

They brought Daniel before the king and asked the king whether it was true that he had made a law that no one could kneel down to anyone except to him.

The king answered that this was his law and it could not be changed. So all the governors told the king that Daniel had broken the law and that he must be punished.

The king was very upset when he heard about this. He liked and trusted Daniel and he wanted to save him, but he could not change the law. So he ordered Daniel to be sent to the lions' den. Yet, as he was sent away, the king said to him, "May your God save you."

Daniel was locked in the lions' den all night. The king arose early the next morning and went to the lions' den. When he arrived, he found Daniel standing there unharmed. The king then ordered Daniel's enemies to be thrown into that same lions' den. The lions immediately attacked Daniel's enemies and ate them up. When the king saw how God had spared Daniel and had punished his enemies, he, too, praised the greatness of the Lord.

The angel Gabriel appears to Zechariah.

THE REVELATION TO ZECHARIAH

Luke 1:4-18

THE Jews of the Old Testament had a long, difficult history as they tried to follow the Lord. Often they would sin and turn away from God.

They would worship pagan gods and turn away from their holy traditions. They would also treat the poor and the widows and orphans terribly, failing to care for them in spite of the fact that they were God's chosen ones.

In those times, the Lord would hand them over into the power of their enemies. They would then realize that they had sinned and they would turn back to the Lord. God would forgive them and once again show them His blessings.

Yet the Jewish people knew that there had to be something more. They were waiting for that day when the Lord would show His love to Israel in a special way. They had read what the prophets had said, and they believed that all the prophets were speaking about the same thing: that the Lord was going to send His anointed one, a Messiah, who would lead Israel in the ways of the Lord.

Two of the people who were filled with hope for the coming of the Messiah were Zechariah, a priest in the temple of the Lord, and Elizabeth his wife.

Their stories are told at the beginning of the New Testament, but they also mark the end of the Old Testament. That is why they are placed here in this book.

Zechariah and Elizabeth lived in a small town in the hill country not far from Jerusalem. Elizabeth was also a cousin of Mary, who was to be the mother of Jesus. Both Zechariah and Elizabeth had never had any children and now that they were very old, there was no longer any hope that they could have children.

There were many priests in Israel, and each one of them belonged to a family of priests. Each family would go up to the temple twice a year for a week each time to perform the sacrifices and lead the prayers of the people of God.

When the week of Zechariah's service arrived, he traveled up to Jerusalem. Each day the priests cast lots to see who would offer the incense, and one day the lot fell to Zechariah.

He entered the sanctuary of the temple to offer incense to the Lord while outside the people lifted up their prayers to God. All of a sudden, an angel appeared to him standing on the right side of the altar of incense.

Zechariah was filled with fear when he saw the angel. He did not know what to make of this.

But the angel spoke to him and said, "Do not be frightened, Zechariah. Your prayer has been heard. Your wife Elizabeth shall bear a son whom you shall name John. Joy and gladness will be yours, and many will rejoice at his birth; he will be great in the eyes of the Lord."

The angel explained to Zechariah that his son was never to drink wine or strong drink, for he was to be consecrated to the Lord. The angel said, "He will be filled with the Holy Spirit from his mother's womb."

He also explained to Zechariah that this child would be a new Elijah for his people. This baby would bring many of the children of Israel back to the Lord, for "God Himself will go before him, in the spirit and power of Elijah, to turn the hearts of fathers to their children and the rebellious to the wishes of the just, and to prepare for the Lord a people well-disposed."

Zechariah was confused by all this, for he was very old. He did not think it was possible for him and his wife ever to have children.

But the angel answered that his name was Gabriel and he was so important that he always stood in God's presence. God Himself had sent him to bring this good news to Zechariah and Elizabeth.

Zechariah and Elizabeth prepare for their child.

ZECHARIAH AND ELIZABETH

Luke 1:19-80

GABRIEL proclaimed that because Zechariah had doubted that the Lord would work this wonder, he would be unable to speak until this child was born. The angel then disappeared from his sight.

The people outside the sanctuary began to wonder what was taking Zechariah so long. When he finally came out and was unable to speak, they realized that something very mysterious had happened. He was only able to explain what had happened by making signs.

When the week of Zechariah's service as priest was over, he returned to his home. A short time later, Elizabeth, his wife, discovered that she was going to have a baby. She was truly filled with joy and thanked God for His wonderful gift.

The child who would be born to Zechariah and Elizabeth, John the Baptist, would be an important messenger of the Lord. He would prepare the way of the Lord, for the sacred time had arrived when God would send His own holy Son to this world to set us free from our sins.

THE NEW TESTAMENT

THE New Testament is both a continuation of the story that we have already seen in the Old Testament and something very new.

In the Old Testament we saw how God called a people to Himself and how He made a covenant of love with that people. He promised that He would always be with them.

God never turns back on His promises, even when we turn away from Him with our sins. The New Testament is the story of how God defeated the power of sin through the life and death of His only Son.

Jesus was born one like us in a cave in Bethlehem. He went about proclaiming that the kingdom of God was near, and He called us to turn back to God with all our heart, soul, and strength. He called the apostles and disciples to follow Him and to share in His mission. He gave us a new set of laws, the beatitudes, which challenge us to be as loving and merciful as God is. And then on Calvary He took up His cross and died for us, sealing His new promise, the new covenant, with His own blood.

Even then, His love knew no limit. God the Father raised Jesus from the dead so that death could no longer have power over Him and so that we could have the promise that one day we will rise with Jesus. He then sent His Holy Spirit to fill us with His life, making us into a Church.

The angel Gabriel greets Mary.

THE ANNUNCIATION

Luke 1:26-38

THE time had arrived for God to fulfill the promises that He had made through the prophets.

The Lord sent the angel Gabriel to speak to a young woman named Mary from the town of Nazareth. Mary was engaged to a man named Joseph, a carpenter from that same town, but they had not yet begun to live together. In those days, a man and a woman would become engaged about a year before they began to live together.

The angel greeted Mary saying, "Hail, Mary, full of grace, the Lord is with you." Mary was surprised and confused by this greeting for she did not understand what it meant.

Gabriel continued, "Do not fear, Mary. You have found favor with God. You shall conceive and bear a son and give Him the name Jesus (a name which means 'Yahweh saves'). Great will be His dignity and He shall be called Son of the Most High. The Lord will give Him the throne of David His father. He will rule over the house of Jacob forever and His reign will be without end."

Mary had been confused before, but now she was deeply troubled. She had agreed to marry Joseph, but they were not yet living together. Mary was still a virgin, and so she had no idea of how she could be pregnant. She said to the angel, "How can this be since I do not know man?"

The angel replied, "The Holy Spirit will come upon you and the power of the Most High will overshadow you. Therefore, the child to be born will be called the holy Son of God."

The angel also explained to Mary that her cousin, Elizabeth, was pregnant and was now in her sixth month. Mary realized that this was a great miracle, for she knew that Elizabeth was far too old to have children. Yet God had blessed her and given her this gift, for, as the angel said, "nothing is impossible with God."

Having heard this, Mary now knew that God was working great miracles, and she realized that God had chosen her for a holy mission. So she responded, "I am the servant of the Lord. Let it be done to me as you say."

The angel then disappeared, and Mary was left alone. She must have been very frightened by all that had happened and all that had been said. Yet she decided to trust in the Lord and she placed herself in God's hands.

She must also have wondered how she would ever explain all of these things to Joseph.

THE VISITATION

Luke 1:39-80

NOW Joseph knew the law of the Lord, and he was greatly troubled. His wife had been found to be pregnant, and according to the law he could have sent her out to be stoned. Yet Joseph was a just and kind man, and he did not want to subject Mary to this horrible punishment. He decided that he would divorce her quietly, telling Mary's parents that he would no longer marry her.

But that night Joseph had a dream. An angel of the Lord appeared to him and said, "Joseph, son of David, have no fear about taking Mary as your wife. It is by the power of the Holy Spirit that she has conceived this child. She is to have a son and you are to name Him Jesus because He will save His people from their sins."

When Joseph heard this message, he immediately obeyed the command of the Lord. He knew that the prophets had spoken about this child.

One of the great prophets, Isaiah, had said, "The young maiden shall be with child and give birth to a son and they shall call him Emmanuel." That name means, "God is with us," and Joseph now knew that this message was being fulfilled.

So Joseph took Mary home to his house, and they lived together from that day on, but Mary remained a virgin.

Mary did not think of herself during all these difficulties. She hurried off to the hill country of Judea where Zechariah and Elizabeth lived so that she could help Elizabeth until her child was born.

When Elizabeth heard Mary's greeting, she was filled with joy. The baby leapt for joy in her womb. Filled with the Holy Spirit, Elizabeth cried out, "Blest are you among women and blest is the fruit of your womb. But who am I that the mother of my Lord should come to me? The moment your greeting sounded in my ears, the baby leapt in my womb for joy. Blest is she who trusted that the Lord's words would be fulfilled."

Mary stayed with Elizabeth until her child was born. When it came time to name the child, they asked Elizabeth what name he would have. She answered that his name would be John.

The people were confused by this, for no one in their family was named John. So they asked Zechariah what he would call his son. Zechariah called for a tablet and wrote down, "His name is John."

From that moment on Zechariah could speak. He praised the Lord for His goodness to them. The people were filled with fear, because they knew that God was working great miracles in their midst.

The baby leaps in Elizabeth's womb when Mary arrives.

Mary and Joseph are filled with joy at the birth of Jesus.

JESUS IS BORN

Luke 2:1-20

AS the time for Mary to have her child approached, Mary and Joseph faced one more difficulty. The emperor of the Roman Empire, Caesar Augustus, had ordered that a census was to be taken over the whole world. All people were to travel to the cities and towns of their ancestors so that a record might be made of their names and what they owned.

Joseph and Mary belonged to the tribe of Judah, to the family of David. And so they traveled to the city of David, to Bethlehem, a small town not far from Jerusalem. This was a very difficult journey for Mary, for she was almost ready to have her child, but again she trusted in the Lord.

When they arrived in Bethlehem, Joseph went off looking for a place for them to stay, but there were so many people who had traveled there for the census that there was no place for them to stay.

Finally, Joseph stopped at an inn and told them that he had to find a place for his wife to stay, for she was about to have her child. The people who owned the inn felt sorry for Mary, so they told Joseph that he could take Mary to a cave outside the town where the animals were kept during the bad weather.

Mary and Joseph went to the cave, and Mary had her child there. They cleaned out a manger, the place where hay is placed for the animals, and they laid the baby Jesus in it.

Mary wrapped Jesus in a cloth to keep Him warm. They thanked God for the wonderful gift He had given them.

At that time there were some shepherds in the fields watching their flocks. An angel appeared to them and proclaimed, "You have nothing to fear! I come to proclaim good news to you and tidings of great joy to be shared by the whole people. This day in David's city a Savior has been born to you, the Messiah and Lord." The angel told the shepherds that they would find the baby wrapped in a cloth, just as Mary had done.

Suddenly the sky was filled with angels singing, "Glory to God in high heaven, peace on earth to those on whom His favor rests."

After the angels departed, the shepherds went in haste to visit the child and found everything as the angels had told them. They told Mary and Joseph what the angels had said to them.

All were filled with wonder and they gave praise to the Lord for all that they had seen and heard. Mary kept all of these things in her heart.

THE PRESENTATION

Luke 2:22-40

ON the eighth day after Jesus was born, Joseph and Mary had Him circumcised. They gave Him the name Jesus, the name that the angel had spoken to them before He was born.

Forty days after Jesus had been born, it was time for Mary to go to the temple to be purified. She went with Joseph and the baby Jesus. They presented their offering to the Lord, the offering that was to be given by those who were poor: two turtledoves.

While they were in the temple, they met a man named Simeon. He was a good and holy Jewish man who had prayed all his life that he might see the one whom God was going to send.

The Holy Spirit had revealed to Simeon that God would answer his prayer, for he would not die until he had seen the Messiah with his own eyes.

That morning the Holy Spirit had inspired Simeon to come to the temple to pray. He met Joseph and Mary as they were carrying their baby, and he was filled with a spirit of joy.

Simeon took the baby in his arms and prayed, "Now, Master, You can dismiss Your servant in peace; You have fulfilled Your word. For my eyes have witnessed Your saving deed displayed for all the people to see: a revealing light to the Gentiles, the glory of Your people Israel."

Simeon was so happy because he knew this baby was the promised one of God for whom he had waited so long. Even if he were to die at that very moment, he would certainly die a happy man, for his life was now filled with meaning.

Mary and Joseph were filled with wonder when they heard what Simeon had said. Simeon blessed them and then told Mary that Jesus would be a great sign for the people of Israel.

Jesus would call people to follow God, and while some would say yes, others would say no. Those who said yes would rise with the Lord, but those who said no would fall.

He then spoke directly to Mary and told her that a sword would pierce her heart. Mary would feel the pain of her heart breaking as she saw her only son suffer, but she would always continue to trust in God.

A holy woman named Anna also came up and gave witness to the goodness of the Lord. She gave thanks to God for having seen the child and she spoke about Him to all those people in Jerusalem who awaited the promised one of the Lord.

Mary and Joseph bring the baby Jesus to the temple.

The three wise men give honor to Jesus.

THE THREE WISE MEN

Matthew 2:1-12

AROUND the time that Jesus was born a star rose in the sky, indicating that a new king had been born to the Jewish people. Three wise men in the east saw the star and understood its meaning. They traveled from the east to give honor to this newborn king.

When they arrived in Jerusalem, they asked around to see if anyone knew where they might find the new king of the Jews. The people were un able to give them an answer because they did not know. Some of those whom they asked reported to Herod that three strangers were there looking for a new king.

Now, Herod was a very evil man. He would kill anyone who threatened to take away his throne. He called the wise men and the priests of the Jewish people together and asked them where this new king was supposed to be born.

All the Jewish wise men studied the sayings of the prophets and returned with the answer that the Messiah was to be born in Bethlehem. It was written in the book of the prophet Micah, "And you, Bethlehem, land of Judah, are by no means least among the princes of Judah, since from you shall come a ruler who is to shepherd My people Israel."

Herod then called the wise men from the east to his palace and spoke with them. He asked them exactly when the star had first appeared. He wanted to find out as much information as possible, for he was planning to harm the child Jesus. He was afraid that Jesus would take away his kingdom.

The king sent the three wise men on their way, telling them to return to him after they had found the child. He told them that he wanted to know where the child was so that he could honor Him. He really wanted to know where Jesus was so that he could kill Him.

The moment that the three wise men left the palace, they once again saw the star that had led them there. It stood still over the place where the child was to be found.

They entered the house and saw Mary holding the child. They bowed down to Jesus and presented Him with gifts they had brought. One had brought gold, a gift one would give to a king. Another had brought frank-incense, an incense to be burned to God. The third had brought myrrh, an ointment to be used for those who had died, for Jesus would save us from our sins through His death.

Joseph takes Mary and the child and flees into Egypt.

THE FLIGHT INTO EGYPT

Matthew 1:12-23

ALTHOUGH the three wise men had been told by Herod that they were to return to his palace and tell him all about the child who had been born, they decided not to do this. They received a warning in a dream that Herod planned to harm the child, so they returned home another way.

Soon after Joseph had a dream. In it an angel told him that the child was in danger, for Herod sought to kill Him. Joseph was to take Mary and Jesus and flee down to Egypt. Joseph obeyed the message he had received and took Mary and Jesus down to safety in Egypt.

In the meantime, Herod realized that he had been tricked by the three wise men. He now knew that they had no intention of returning to his palace. Yet he already knew that the Messiah had been born in Bethlehem and he knew just about when He had been born (for he had asked the three wise men when they had first seen the star that announced Jesus' birth).

So Herod ordered that all young boys two years old or younger in Bethlehem and in the surrounding countryside should be put to death.

The soldiers came and took all the young children in that whole region and they put all the boys two years old and younger to death. There was great weeping from the mothers of these children. But Herod and the soldiers would show no mercy, for Herod wanted to kill anyone who might take away his power.

Joseph, Mary, and Jesus settled in Egypt and lived there in peace until the day that King Herod died. When he died, an angel of the Lord appeared to Joseph in a dream to tell him that it was now safe for them to return from Egypt, for Herod was dead.

Joseph took Mary and the child and they traveled back to the land of Israel. On the way, they heard that one of Herod's sons had become the king of Judea, and he was as cruel as his father. Joseph received another warning in a dream that it was not safe to return to Bethlehem, so he took the child and His mother to the region of Galilee which lay to the north. They settled in the town of Nazareth where Joseph worked as a carpenter. All the while Jesus continued to grow in wisdom and in grace.

JESUS IS FOUND IN THE TEMPLE

Luke 2:41-52

JOSEPH and Mary were good Jewish parents, and so every year they would take Jesus up with them to Jerusalem for the feast of Passover. When Jesus was twelve years old, they went up again as was their custom. This was a special trip for Jesus, for a Jewish boy was considered to be a man when he turned twelve years old.

When the feast ended, Mary and Joseph began to travel back to their home in Nazareth. At first they traveled separately and each of them thought that Jesus was with the other one.

When they finally got together, they realized that Jesus was not with either one of them. Yet they just assumed that He was with one of their friends or relatives. They traveled for a full day, but He still did not show up.

So Mary and Joseph began to ask their relatives and friends if anyone had seen their Son. They asked everyone, but no one had seen Jesus since they had left Jerusalem. By now they were very worried; so they turned around and went back to Jerusalem.

When they arrived in the city, they had a difficult time finding Jesus. Finally they went into the temple and were surprised to find Him standing among the teachers of the law. He was listening to all their arguments and asking them questions. All who saw Him were amazed at His intelligence and at His answers.

Mary and Joseph were very surprised to find Him in the temple, and Mary said to Him, "Son, why have You done this to us? You see that Your father and I have been searching for You in sorrow." But Jesus answered His mother, "Why did you search for Me? Did you not know I had to be in My Father's house?"

Jesus was telling them that He had to serve the will of God, His Father, for Jesus was the only Son of God. But they did not fully understand these things until much later when the Holy Spirit made all things clear to them.

Jesus went down with Mary and Joseph to their home in Nazareth. He obeyed them in all things and grew in wisdom and grace before the Lord. Mary kept praying about all these holy things that had happened for she wanted to trust in God's will.

Joseph taught Jesus how to work with wood, for he was a carpenter. They lived a simple life, thanking God for all the good things they had received from the Lord.

Jesus remained at home taking care of Mary, His mother, until He was about thirty years old.

The elders of the Jews are astonished at the wisdom of Jesus.

John baptizes Jesus in the Jordan River.

THE BAPTISM OF JESUS

Matthew 3:1-17; Mark 1:1-11; Luke 3:1-22; John 1:19-34

WHEN Jesus was about thirty years old, it was time for Him to go out and to preach the good news. He traveled down to the region around the Jordan River so that He could be baptized by John the Baptist.

John had gone out to this region to preach to the people that they had to turn back to the Lord. He wore clothes made of camel skin and he ate locusts and wild honey. He continuously fasted and prayed to the Lord.

John knew that he was preparing the way for the One whom God would send. So he invited people to turn away from their evil ways. When they asked him what they should do, he told them, "Let the person with two coats give to the one who has none. The person who has food should do the same." In other words, he told the people to share with whoever did not have enough to eat or drink or wear.

Some tax collectors came up and asked him what they should do to serve the Lord. He gave them a simple answer that they should ask for nothing more in taxes than what they were owed.

Likewise some soldiers came up and asked what they should do. He told them not to be mean to anyone, nor to steal anything. They should simply treat people fairly.

John proclaimed that there was another one coming after him who was greater than he was. He said that he was not worthy to untie that person's sandal strap. He also said that while he was baptizing in water, the One to come would baptize in fire and the Holy Spirit.

Some of the people thought that John himself was the Messiah, but John firmly told them that he was not. He said that he was only the friend of the bridegroom, the best man. Jesus was the one who would marry the Church.

And so Jesus came up to him one day and asked to be baptized. John was confused, for he knew that Jesus was much holier than he. John told Him that Jesus should be baptizing him and not he baptizing Jesus. But Jesus told John that this was the way it should be, for they were to fulfill all of God's commands.

When John had poured the water over Jesus' head, the skies above Him opened up and the Spirit of the Lord descended upon Him in the form of a dove. Then there was a voice that came from the heavens and said, "This is My beloved Son. My favor rests on Him."

The devil tempts Jesus in the desert.

THE TEMPTATION IN THE DESERT

Matthew 4:1-11; Mark 1:12-13; Luke 4:1-13

AFTER Jesus had been baptized, the Spirit led Jesus out into the desert where He fasted and prayed for forty days and forty nights.

While Jesus was in the desert, Satan visited Him to tempt Him. Satan knew that Jesus had already fasted a long time and that He was hungry. He wanted to get Jesus to use His power for His own comfort, for that would be a selfish thing to do. So Satan said to Jesus, "If You are the Son of God, command these stones to turn into bread."

Jesus would have had no trouble changing stones into bread, and He was very hungry. Yet, He was not tricked by Satan's words. He responded, "Scripture has it: 'Not on bread alone is man to live but on every word that comes from the mouth of God.' " In other words, Jesus would trust in God. He did not have to be selfish and use His power in the wrong way. He believed that God would take care of Him.

Next the devil took Jesus off to the holy city. He placed Him on the wall of the temple and told Him, "If You are the Son of God, throw Yourself down. Scripture has it: 'He will bid His angels take care of You; with their hands they will support You that You may never stumble on a stone.' "

The reason that Satan was saying these things was that he saw that Jesus trusted in God, but he thought that maybe he could get Jesus to do something foolish. He wanted Jesus to doubt for just a second, so that Jesus would try to make God prove that He would take care of Him. But Jesus would not play that game. He told the devil, "Scripture also has it: 'You shall not put the Lord your God to the test.' "

A third time the devil tempted Jesus. He took Him to the top of a very high mountain and showed Him all the kingdoms of the world. He told Jesus that he would give Him all these kingdoms if only Jesus would worship him.

Again, Satan was trying to tempt Jesus, telling Him that He should seek honor and power. Instead, Jesus only sought to serve His Father and to serve us. So Jesus said to him,

"Away with you, Satan! Scripture has it, 'You shall honor the Lord your God. Him alone shall you adore.' "

With this Satan fled away, and the Lord sent His angels to care for Jesus. After Jesus had been tempted, He returned from the desert to be with His disciples.

Mary asks Jesus to help the wedding couple.

THE WEDDING FEAST AT CANA

John 2:1-12

IT was only a short time after Jesus had returned from the desert that He shared in a joyous occasion.

Mary had been invited to a wedding feast in the town of Cana, and Jesus and His disciples went along with her. These parties usually lasted several days, and everyone would sing and dance and celebrate the couple's joy.

During the feast, Mary noticed that they had run out of wine. This would have been a very great embarrassment for the families of the man and the woman who were getting married; so Mary went over and told Jesus that they had run out of wine.

Jesus answered, "Woman, how does this concern of yours involve Me? My hour has not yet come."

Although this might sound a little bit as if Jesus were showing disrespect to His mother, this is not what He was doing. This is only the way people spoke to each other in those days.

Jesus was trying to tell His mother that the time for Him to show His love and power had not yet come. That moment when He would show His love was at the Last Supper and on the cross.

But Mary knew that Jesus would not let them down. She told the servants who were waiting on the tables to do whatever Jesus told them to do.

Jesus noticed that there were six large stone jars there. These jars were used to hold water so that all the guests could wash themselves before they would begin to eat. Each of the jars held between twenty and thirty gallons. Now they were almost empty, for the water had been used up.

Jesus told the servants to fill the jars up with water. They did this, filling them up to the brim.

When the servants returned, Jesus told them to take a bit of the water and give it to the headwaiter to taste. When the headwaiter tasted the water, it had become wine.

The headwaiter did not know where the wine had come from, for only the waiters knew that. So he called the groom over and told him that people usually serve the better wine first and then the poorer wine. But the groom had done the opposite, saving the best wine for last, for the water had become a very good wine.

This was the first miracle that Jesus performed. Many of His disciples believed in Him because they saw the wonders that He could do.

A GREAT CATCH OF FISH

Luke 5:1-11

ONE day Jesus was standing on the shore of the Sea of Galilee. There was a large crowd of those who hoped to hear Him speak, for they wanted to hear the Word of God. They all pressed in closer to be able to hear Him.

While He was there, He saw two boats that were pulled up to the shore. The fishermen who worked the boats had gotten out and were washing their nets.

Jesus got into one of the boats, the one that belonged to Peter. He asked Peter to pull out from shore a short distance. When they reached the right spot, they stopped. Jesus remained sitting in the boat while He taught the crowd standing on the shore.

When He had finished teaching the crowd, Jesus had Peter pull away from the shore and head for the deeper water. He told him that he should toss the nets out to fish for a catch.

Peter replied that he and his companions had already been fishing all that night, and they had not been able to catch anything. It did not make any sense to go out again and waste their time.

But Peter said that if Jesus wanted him to try once again, he would.

Peter and the other fishermen tossed out their nets, and when they pulled them in, they could not believe what they saw. The nets were so filled with fish that they were almost breaking.

Peter and the others signaled to their companions in the other boat and called them over to help them with the catch.

When the other boat arrived, they both filled their boats with their fish. The boats were so full that they were both on the point of sinking.

The disciples were all filled with fear when they saw what had happened. Peter fell on his knees before Jesus and said, "Leave me, Lord. I am a sinful man."

Jesus knew what was in Peter's heart, and He wanted him to follow Him.

Jesus said to Peter and the others, "Do not be afraid. From now on you will be catching men and women." Jesus was telling them that they would be searching to bring people to the Lord.

When they heard this, Peter and the others left their boats and everything else that they owned. They abandoned all and followed Jesus to become His disciples.

The apostles catch an incredible number of fish.

Jesus heals the man who was crippled.

JESUS HEALS THE CRIPPLED MAN

Matthew 9:1-8; Mark 2:1-12; Luke 5:17-26

JESUS was teaching the crowd, and He felt called by the Spirit to heal those who were ill and hurting. There were many Pharisees and teachers of the law who came to listen to His teaching.

Those who were following Jesus were all crowded into a house. There were so many of them that there was no room at the door for anyone to get in or out.

While they were there, some men carried one of their friends so that they might lay him before Jesus. The man whom they brought was paralyzed. He could not move at all.

When they arrived at the house, they realized that there was no way for them to carry their friend into the house. So they lifted him up to the roof and began to remove some of the tiles. They made a hole in the middle of the roof and lowered their friend through the hole.

When the people saw someone being lowered through the roof, they all looked to see what would happen next.

Jesus spoke to the man and said, "My friend, your sins are forgiven you." The man was filled with joy. He knew that the thing that was most painful for him had been healed.

But the teachers of the law and the Pharisees were angry. They began to ask each other how Jesus could forgive sins, for only God can forgive sins. They were not happy that the man had found peace; they only wanted to argue with Jesus.

Jesus knew what they were thinking and saying. So He asked them, "Why do you have such thoughts? Which is easier to say, 'Your sins are forgiven you,' or to say, 'Get up and walk'?"

Jesus then said that in order to show them that He had the power to forgive sins, He would heal the man. He told the man, "I say to you, get up! Take your mat with you, and return to your house."

The man immediately stood up before all of them. He picked up his mat and went on his way, praising the Lord all the way home for the mercy that had been shown to him.

All who saw this miracle were filled with wonder. They began to praise God and they said to each other, "Truly we have seen wonderful things today." All then knew that Jesus did have the power to forgive sins.

THE SERMON ON THE MOUNT

Matthew 5:1—7:29

MANY people very often gathered together to listen to Jesus' teaching. One day Jesus climbed up on a mountain and had the people sit down to listen to Him.

He gave them a new set of commandments. The ten commandments had only told the people what they should do or not do. They were the absolute minimum of what one had to do to avoid being cut off from God. These new commandments, called the *beatitudes*, invited people to do far more. They called people to be good and loving. Jesus said:

How blest are the poor in spirit: the reign of God is theirs.
Blest too are the sorrowing; they shall be consoled.
Blest are the lowly; they shall inherit the land.
Blest are they who hunger and thirst for holiness; they shall have their fill.
Blest are they who show mercy; mercy shall be theirs.
Blest are the single-hearted for they shall see God.
Blest too the peacemakers; they shall be called children of God.
Blest are those persecuted for holiness' sake; the reign of God is theirs.
Blest are you when they insult you and persecute you and utter every kind of slander against you because of Me.
Be glad and rejoice, for your reward is great in heaven; they persecuted the prophets before you in the very same way.

Later the apostles asked Jesus to teach them how to pray. He taught them a prayer that helps us to place our trust in God, our Father. (Known as the Lord's Prayer, it has become a favorite Christian prayer.) Jesus said:

Our Father in heaven,
    hallowed be Your Name,
    Your kingdom come,
    Your will be done,
        on earth as it is in heaven.
    Give us today our daily bread;
    Forgive us our sins,
        as we forgive those who sin against us.
    Save us from the time of trial
        and deliver us from evil.

Jesus instructs the disciples and crowds on the mountain.

The centurion asks Jesus to heal his servant boy.

THE CENTURION

Matthew 8:5-13; Luke 7:1-10; John 4:46-54

AS Jesus was entering the city of Capernaum, He was met by a centurion, a Roman army official who was in charge of 100 soldiers.

The centurion said to Jesus, "Sir, my serving boy is at home in bed paralyzed, suffering painfully." Jesus said to the centurion, "I will come and cure him." But the centurion said to Jesus, "Sir, I am not worthy to have You under my roof. Just give an order and my boy will get better." The centurion explained to Jesus that he knew what it meant to give an order. He could say to one soldier, "Come here," and the soldier would come. He could say to another, "Go there," and the soldier would go.

Jesus turned to the Jews who were following Him and said to them, "I assure you, I have never found this much faith in Israel."

Jesus then said to the centurion, "Go home. It shall be done because you trusted." When the centurion arrived home, he found that the servant had been healed that very moment.

THE WIDOW OF NAIM

Luke 7:11-17

SOON after this, Jesus and those who were traveling with Him arrived at a town named Naim. As they approached the gate of the town, they saw that there was a funeral procession heading out from the town. Asking around, Jesus discovered that the person who had died was the only son of a widow. When Jesus heard this and saw all the people who had joined the funeral procession, He felt very sorry for her. He knew that this widow would now have no one to take care of her in her old age.

Jesus walked up to the mother who had lost her son and said to her, "Do not cry." Then he walked over to the men who were carrying the body. He told them to stop, and they halted their procession. He then said, "Young man, I bid you get up." The man who had died came back to life, and Jesus gave him to this mother.

The people were filled with fear when they saw this great miracle. They said, "A great prophet has risen among us," and "God has visited His people."

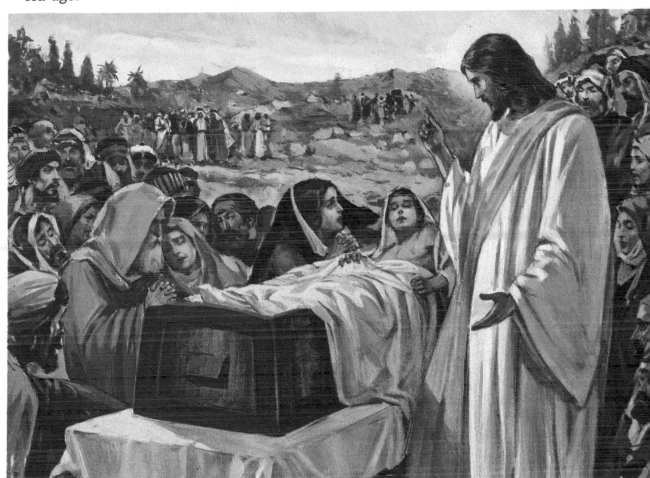

Jesus raises the son of the widow of Naim.

THE CALMING OF THE STORM

Matthew 8:23-27; Mark 4:35-41; Luke 8:22-25

ONE day Jesus got into a boat with His disciples and headed across the Sea of Galilee. Some of His disciples were fishermen, so they knew how to sail their boats well. While they were busy with the sails, Jesus fell asleep. He was tired for people were always asking Him to teach or to do a favor, and this trip across the sea gave Him a few moments of rest.

The Sea of Galilee could be a very dangerous place to sail a boat. One moment the sea was so calm that the water appeared to be made of glass, and then suddenly a storm could arise that would cause huge waves to come crashing over the boats. Many boats had been lost when they had gotten caught in the middle of the sea during one of those storms.

While Jesus and His disciples were crossing the sea, one of these terrible storms suddenly arose. The disciples were filled with fear, because it seemed certain that the boat would sink. Yet Jesus was still asleep.

They called out to Jesus to wake Him up, saying, "Master, master, we are lost." He woke up and ordered the wind and the waves to be quiet. They were immediately calm. He then said to the disciples, "Where is your faith?"

They were filled with fear and admiration and said to each other, "What sort of man can this be who commands even the winds and the sea and they obey Him?"

Another time the disciples were crossing the sea alone while Jesus stayed on shore to pray. In the middle of the night a great storm arose and they feared for their lives.

All at once, they saw Jesus walking across the water. They were sure that it was a ghost, but He told them to be calm for it was He.

Peter called out to the Lord and said, "Lord, if it is really You, tell me to come to You across the water." Jesus said, "Come," and Peter got out of the boat and began to walk toward Jesus on the water.

But Peter heard how strong the wind was and he began to doubt. As his faith wavered, he began to sink and cried out, "Lord, save me." Jesus stretched out His hand and saved him. He then asked Peter why his faith had weakened. At that moment, the wind and the waves died down.

Jesus calms the wind and the waves.

THE DAUGHTER OF JAIRUS

Matthew 9:18-26; Mark 5:21-43; Luke 8:40-56

JESUS traveled all around the Sea of Galilee, even into the territory of the pagans. Once when He was returning from pagan territory, He was met by a crowd that was waiting for Him.

A certain man named Jairus, who was the leader of his synagogue, came up to Jesus and fell on his knees before Him. He begged Jesus to come with him to his home for his little daughter, who was about twelve years old, was dying. So Jesus followed him to go to his house.

The crowd was very great and people were pressing in from every side. In the crowd there was a woman who had been sick for twelve years. Many doctors had tried to cure her, but she just kept getting worse and worse.

The woman thought to herself that if only she could touch the hem of Jesus' robe, she would get well. She reached in from the midst of the crowd pressing in on Jesus and touched His robe. The second she touched it, she got well.

Jesus could feel that the power of healing had gone out from Him and He turned around and said, "Who touched Me?" His disciples looked at Him as if He were crazy. They exclaimed that the crowd was pressing in on Him from every side and He wanted to know who touched Him! But Jesus insisted that someone had touched Him.

The woman realized that she could not hide; so she came forward shaking with fear. She fell on her knees and explained to Him why she had touched Him. Jesus was pleased and said to her, "Daughter, it is your faith that has cured you. Now go in peace."

They had just started on their way again when a messenger came forward and told them not to bother Jesus for the girl had already died. But Jesus said that they should still trust and she would live.

When they arrived at the house, He took only the girls' parents with Peter, John, and James inside. They were met by people crying for the girl, but He told them to stop crying for she was only asleep. These people laughed at Him when He said this. For they knew she was dead.

Jesus went over and took the girl by the hand and said to her, "Little girl, get up." She immediately came back to life. He told them to give her something to eat.

Everyone who heard of this miracle was filled with wonder.

Jesus brings the daughter of Jairus back to life.

Jesus calls the twelve to be His apostles.

THE MISSION OF THE APOSTLES

Matthew 10:1-42; Mark 3:13-19; 6:7-13; Luke 6:12-16; 9:2-5

JESUS slowly began to gather more and more followers. Some of them followed Him on their own while others were called in a special way.

Peter, Andrew, James, and John, for example, had been called from their nets on the Sea of Galilee. Matthew, on the other hand, had been a tax collector. Jesus came up to him one day and said, "Follow Me." Matthew left everything he had and followed Jesus. He even threw a party with all his friends invited to celebrate the fact that Jesus had called him.

At a certain point, Jesus decided that He would call twelve of His disciples in a special way and name them apostles, a word that means "those sent." They would be the leaders of His Church, the New Israel.

So Jesus went up a mountain to pray and He spent the night with the Father. The next morning He came down the mountain and named the twelve apostles.

There was Simon, to whom He gave the name Peter (which means rock, for he was the rock on which Jesus would build the Church) and Peter's brother, Andrew.

There were the sons of Zebedee, James and John, who were both fishermen.

There were Philip and Bartholomew.

There were Matthew, the tax collector, and Thomas, the one who would doubt Jesus' resurrection.

There were James, the son of Alphaeus, and Simon, who belonged to the Zealot party.

Finally, there were Judas, the son of James, whom we now call Jude, and Judas Iscariot, who betrayed our Lord.

Jesus sent them out with power and authority to conquer all kinds of demons and to cure diseases. They were to proclaim the kingdom of God. He told them, "Take nothing for the journey, neither walking staff nor traveling bag; no bread, no money. No one is to have two coats. Stay at whatever house you enter and proceed from there. When people will not receive you, leave that town and shake its dust from your feet as a testimony against them."

Another time Jesus sent a larger group, seventy-two disciples, off to preach. He sent them out two by two, telling them that He was sending them like lambs in the midst of wolves.

Both times, those who had been sent came back rejoicing for they had been able to do great miracles. Jesus reminded them that the miracles were not the important thing, but rather the fact that they were one with God.

THE MULTIPLICATION OF LOAVES AND FISHES

Matthew 14:13-21; Mark 6:32-44; Luke 9:10-17; John 6:1-15

WHEN the apostles returned from their mission, they told Jesus all that they had done. He took them aside so that He could speak with them in private, but the people who had been following Jesus heard about this and followed them.

Jesus stopped there and taught them at length about the kingdom of God. He also healed all who were in need of healing.

As sunset drew near, the twelve came up to Jesus because they were worried. There were many, many people there, and there was hardly any food, for they were in a deserted spot.

The apostles told Jesus that He should dismiss the crowd so that they could go off to the towns and farms nearby to buy some food for themselves and to find a place to spend the night.

Jesus answered the apostles with a question, "Why do you not give them something to eat yourselves?" This question confused the apostles, for they had hardly any food of their own and the crowd following them was enormous; there were well over five thousand people.

How could they hope to get enough food to give even a small portion to each person! They told Jesus, "We have nothing but five loaves and two fish. Or shall we ourselves go and buy food for all these people?"

They asked this even though they knew that Jesus would never send them to buy food for the crowd. First of all, they did not have enough money. But even if they did have more money, it would have taken them days to gather enough to feed all these people.

Jesus told His disciples, "Have them sit down in groups of fifty or so." When He looked out on the hillside, the people almost appeared to be flower beds scattered among the green grass.

The Lord then took the five loaves and the two fish in His hands. He raised His eyes to the heavens and said a blessing over them. He broke the loaves and the fish and gave them to the people.

A great miracle occurred that day, for Jesus kept breaking that bread and fish until there was enough food for all the people. He had multiplied the loaves and fish so much, in fact, that when all the people had finished eating their fill and they had gathered up all the leftovers, there were twelve baskets of food.

Jesus blesses and multiplies loaves and fishes.

THE TRANSFIGURATION

Matthew 17:1-9; Mark 9:2-10; Luke 9:28-36

ONE day Jesus took Peter, James, and John and climbed up Mount Tabor. When they reached the top of the mountain, they stopped to pray.

While Jesus was praying, His appearance suddenly changed. His face and His clothes became white as wool, as bright as the sun. He was so filled with the power and the glory of God that it was almost as if He were sitting upon the throne of God.

Suddenly the disciples saw that there were two men speaking to Jesus: Moses and Elijah. They, too, were filled with the glory of God. They spoke among themselves of those things that would happen to Jesus when He reached Jerusalem.

The disciples should have realized that Moses and Elijah were there to proclaim that Jesus was the Messiah, for the Jews always spoke of how Elijah would prepare the way for the Messiah and how the Messiah would be even greater than Moses.

But the disciples were filled with wonder at all of the things that were happening.

Peter, James, and John fell into a deep sleep, and when they awoke they saw all three of them, Jesus, Elijah, and Moses, standing in their glory. After a while, Moses and Elijah appeared to be going on their way. Peter was bothered by the fact that they were leaving.

So Peter said to Jesus, "Master, how good it is for us to be here. Let us set up three booths, one for you, one for Moses, and one for Elijah." Peter was so confused by all this that he did not really know what he was saying.

While they were still speaking, a cloud appeared and overshadowed them. The disciples were filled with fear because they did not know what would happen next.

Then from inside the cloud, which marked the presence of God among His people, they heard a voice saying, "This is My Son, My Chosen One. Listen to Him."

When the voice fell silent, they looked up and saw that Jesus was standing there alone.

As they were coming down the mountain, Jesus firmly cautioned them that they were not to tell anyone about this until the Son of Man had been raised from the dead.

Jesus had allowed Peter, James, and John to see these things so that when the time of His suffering and death would arrive, they would understand that this was all God's will. Yet, they did not fully understand all of these things until Jesus rose from the dead.

Jesus, Moses, and Elijah appear in their glory.

The Good Samaritan shows great mercy.

THE GOOD SAMARITAN

Luke 10:29-37

ONE day a lawyer came up to Jesus and asked Him a question. He said, "Teacher, what must I do to have everlasting life?"

Jesus wanted to see whether the man was sincere or whether he was just trying to trick Him, so He asked him, "What is written in the law?"

The man answered, "You shall love the Lord your God with all your heart, with all your soul, with all your strength, and with all your mind, and you shall love your neighbor as yourself."

Jesus said to the man, "You have answered correctly. Do this and you shall live." But the man asked Jesus what did it mean to love one's neighbor. Who was one's neighbor? Was it one's family? Was it the people who lived next door? Maybe it was the people who lived in the same city or country? Or did it mean something else?

Jesus decided that the best way to answer this question was to tell him a story. So Jesus told him the parable of the Good Samaritan.

There was a Jewish man going down from Jerusalem to Jericho. Now the road was very lonely, and not many people passed along it each day.

There were also many caves and hills along the way. These were often hiding places for people who wished to rob those traveling along the road.

Some robbers who were hiding along the road saw the man coming down from Jerusalem. They stopped him and began to beat him up. They stole his donkey, his money, and even his clothes.

The robbers beat the man up so much that he was bleeding and badly hurt. But they refused to show him any mercy. They left him lying half dead by the side of the road.

It happened that a priest was traveling along the same road. He saw the poor man lying on the side of the road, but he would not stop to help him.

We do not know if he refused to stop because he was afraid that the robbers were still lying in wait or if he just could not be bothered. All we know is that he did not stop.

Soon afterward a Levite, a man who helped the priests in the temple, came passing by. He, too, saw the man who had been beaten and robbed lying on the side of the road, but he would not stop. He just continued on his way.

Finally, a Samaritan came passing by. Samaritans usually hated Jews, and Jews usually hated Samaritans. They did not even talk to each other.

Yet, when the Samaritan saw the Jewish man lying on the side of the road, he immediately went over and began to care for him. He poured oil and wine onto his wounds to cleanse them. He then took some of his own clothes and ripped them to make bandages for the man's wounds.

After this, the Samaritan put the man on his donkey and carried him off to the nearest inn. He gave the innkeeper some money to pay him for taking care of the wounded man. He also told the innkeeper that if it cost more than he had given him, he would pay him the rest on his way back.

The Jews were shocked when they heard this story, for they never thought of Samaritans as their neighbors.

But Jesus then asked the lawyer who the man's true neighbor was. The lawyer answered that it was the Samaritan, the one who had treated him with compassion. So Jesus told the lawyer to go and do the same. We should never look at a person's color or race or religion. We should just show every person God's love.

MARTHA AND MARY

Luke 10:38-42; John 12:1-8

JESUS had three very close friends who lived in a village named Bethany, which was not very far from Jerusalem. His friends were two sisters, Martha and Mary, and their brother Lazarus. Whenever Jesus passed that way, He would often stay at their house for the evening.

Once when Jesus was passing that way, He stopped to visit them. Martha had been very busy all day long, for she wanted to make sure that everything was perfect for her guests.

Martha had been cleaning before they had arrived. She had also been cooking all day so that she could serve her guests a very special meal.

All this time while Martha was busy getting things ready for their guests, Mary had been sitting down listening to Jesus teach and speaking with Him.

At first Martha did not think anything of it, but the more she thought about it, the angrier she got. Here she was stuck doing all the work while Mary was just sitting down and relaxing. She was furious that her sister could be so lazy and get away with it.

Eventually she could take it no longer. She went over to Jesus and asked Him to tell Mary that she was being rude for not helping her.

Martha really expected Jesus to take her side. For He was always speaking of serving other people, and that was what Martha thought she was doing and Mary was not.

But Jesus turned to Martha and told her something she did not expect to hear. He said that she was busy with many things, but Mary had chosen the better thing. For while Martha had been running around the house ever since He had arrived, Mary had not stopped spending time with Him.

Another time that Jesus visited their house, Mary took a pound of very expensive perfume and anointed Jesus' feet with it. She then dried His feet with her hair. By doing this, she was showing Jesus great honor and respect.

Judas, who was there, started to complain that the perfume should have been sold to buy food for the poor. He did not do this because he wanted to help the poor, but because he took care of the money and he wanted to steal some of it for himself.

But Jesus told Judas to leave her alone, for she was doing this as a sign of love in preparation for His death and burial. Jesus was trying to tell Judas to worry less about money and more about the person right in front of him, but Judas would not listen.

Jesus blesses Mary who spent time listening to Him.

The Prodigal Son is welcomed by his happy father.

THE PRODIGAL SON

Luke 15:11-32

ANOTHER time Jesus was speaking to the scribes and Pharisees and He wanted to teach them about the mercy of God. So He told them another story, this one about the Prodigal Son.

There was a man who owned a large farm who had two sons. The younger of his sons came up to his father and told him that he did not want to wait until his father died to receive his part of the father's property. He asked his father to give him his share immediately.

The father sold what he had to collect the amount of money that the son would have inherited. He then gave the money to his son.

The son took his money and traveled to a distant land. There he lived a very evil life and wasted all his money on parties and drinking. In a short time he ran out of money.

Then he discovered that all the people who had been his friends while he had been rich had suddenly forgotten who he was. To make things worse, a terrible famine struck that land.

The man had nothing to eat and he was desperate; so he found a job feeding the pigs on a farm. He was miserable, for even then he had hardly anything to eat.

He thought to himself, "This is crazy. Here I am, longing to eat the things I feed to my pigs while my father's workers have more than enough to eat."

So the unhappy man decided to return home and ask for his father's forgiveness.

His father saw him coming from a distance and ran up to him to greet and hug him. The son said, "Father, I have sinned against God and against you. I no longer deserve to be called your son."

But the father ordered his servants to bring beautiful clothes for his son. He also ordered that a great feast be prepared to celebrate the return of his son.

The older brother had been in the field when all this happened. When he was coming in from work that evening, he heard the celebration and asked a servant what was happening.

The servant told the older brother that they were celebrating the return of his brother. He became angry and would not go in.

But the father came out and begged his angry son to come and celebrate, for his younger brother had been lost but now was found; he had been dead and now had come back to life.

This is how God feels when we turn from our sins.

Jesus blesses the children.

JESUS AND THE CHILDREN

Matthew 18:1-5; 19:13-15, Mark 9:33-37, 10:13-16, Luke 9:46-48; 18:15-17

JESUS had a special love for children. He always had time to talk with them or even to play games with them. He always put aside the other things that He was doing to spend time with them.

Once a group of children came to Him so that He would give them His blessing. The disciples knew that Jesus was very tired, and they did not want to bother Him. They tried to chase the children away.

When Jesus saw what they were doing, He became quite angry. He said to them, "Let the children come to Me and do not hinder them. It is to just such as these that the kingdom of heaven belongs! I assure you that whoever does not accept the kingdom of God like a little child shall not take part in it."

Jesus then hugged all the children and placed His hands on their heads, giving them His blessing.

Another time Jesus asked the disciples, "What were you discussing on the way home?"

Suddenly there was a moment of absolute silence, for the disciples were terribly embarrassed. They had been discussing all along the way who was the most important of the twelve.

Jesus told the disciples, "If anyone wishes to rank first, he must remain the least one of all and the servant of all." He then placed a little child in their midst and hugged the child. He told them, "Whoever welcomes a child such as this for My sake welcomes Me. And whoever welcomes Me welcomes, not Me, but Him who sent Me."

In other words, Jesus was telling the disciples that they should be more concerned with loving the little ones of God who need our love than with questions of who was important and who was not.

The only really important person for one who follows Christ is someone who needs our love. Everything else is not really important.

Still another time Jesus spoke about those who gave bad example to children. He was very upset when He thought of how some people taught children how to do evil things, for He loved the fact that children can be so good and innocent.

Jesus said that it would be better for someone to tie a millstone (a huge stone used to grind grain) around his neck and throw himself in the sea rather than give scandal to one of His little ones.

THE RICH YOUNG MAN

Matthew 19:16-22; Mark 10:17-22; Luke 16:19-31; 18:18-23

THERE were many people who were so attached to their money and what they owned that they found it difficult to follow Jesus. They had no room in their lives for Him.

There was a rich young man who wanted to follow Jesus. He went up to Jesus and said, "Good teacher, what must I do to share in everlasting life?"

Jesus said to him, "You know the commandments: You shall not commit adultery. You shall not kill. You shall not steal. You shall not bear false witness. Honor your father and your mother."

The rich young man replied, "I have kept all these since I was a boy."

When Jesus heard this, He felt great love for this man, and so He invited him to give himself totally to the Lord.

Jesus said, "There is one thing further you must do. Sell all you have and give it to the poor. You will have treasure in heaven. Then come and follow Me."

The man became sad, for he had many possessions; he was very rich. He turned away and left Jesus.

Jesus then spoke to the people standing there, saying, "How hard it will be for the rich to enter the kingdom of God! Indeed, it is easier for a camel to go through a needle's eye than for a rich man to enter the kingdom of heaven."

Jesus also told a story of how the rich often forget to share their goods with the poor.

There was a rich man who lived in a fine house and threw great feasts. A poor man named Lazarus lived at the gate to his house. He would have loved to eat the crumbs that fell from the rich man's table, but the rich man never gave him anything.

Both of these men died. Lazarus, the poor man, was taken up into heaven where he found his eternal reward. The rich man was sent to hell where he was punished for his selfishness.

The rich man called up to heaven and asked whether Lazarus could dip his finger in water and drop it down on the rich man's lips to quench his thirst.

God would not allow this, for He told the rich man that there was a great distance between heaven and hell over which no one could pass. Besides, the rich man had received his reward in this life and had not been generous in sharing his goods. Now he must accept his punishment.

The rich young man goes away sad.

Jesus commands Lazarus to rise from the tomb.

JESUS RAISES LAZARUS FROM THE DEAD

John 11:1-44

JESUS had gone down to the area around the Jordan River when He received the news that Lazarus, His friend, was very sick. Lazarus was the brother of Martha and Mary, and Jesus loved them very much. Yet Jesus did not head back to their house right away. He told the disciples who were with Him that this sickness would not end in death but would give glory to God. Then He remained where He was for another two days.

Finally, He told his disciples that it was time to head up to Bethany. The disciples did not like that idea, for only a short time before the Jews had tried to arrest Jesus, and the disciples thought that they might try it again. But Jesus told them that He had to live in the daylight and not sneak around in the night.

Then Jesus told the disciples why He wanted to go up to Bethany. He told them that Lazarus, his friend, had fallen asleep. They were confused, for if he had fallen asleep, surely he would get better from his illness. They had not understood what Jesus really meant; so Jesus said it clearly, "Lazarus is dead."

By the time they arrived in Bethany, Lazarus had already been dead for four days.

When Martha and Mary heard that Jesus had arrived, Martha ran out to greet Him. She said to Him, "Lord, if You had been here, my brother would never have died." Jesus told her, "Your brother will rise again."

Martha thought that He was talking about the resurrection of all the dead at the end of time, and she told Jesus that she believed he would rise then.

But Jesus answered, "I am the resurrection and the life: whoever believes in Me, though he should die, will come to life; and whoever is alive and believes in Me will never die." Jesus asked Martha if she believed, and she answered, "Yes, Lord, I have come to believe that You are the Messiah, the Son of God: He who is to come into the world."

Mary then came out and Jesus told her, too, that He was the resurrection of those who placed faith in Him.

Jesus then went out to the place where Lazarus was buried. He wept, for He loved Lazarus very much.

Jesus then ordered that the stone in front of the tomb be taken off. He lifted up a prayer to the Father and ordered Lazarus to come out of the tomb. Lazarus returned to life and came walking out of the tomb, still bound with the cloth in which he had been buried.

This miracle helped to prepare the people for when Jesus Himself would rise from the dead.

PALM SUNDAY

Matthew 21:1-9; Mark 11:1-10; Luke 19:28-40; John 12:12-19

SHORTLY after this, Jesus was approaching Jerusalem with His disciples. He called two of them over and told them to go into the next town.

There they would find a donkey colt, a young donkey on which no one had ever ridden, which they were to bring to Him. If anyone were to ask why they were taking the animal, they were to answer, "The Master needs it, but He will send it back here at once."

Going into the town, they found the colt tied to a gate, just as Jesus had told them. They untied it and brought it back to Jesus.

Jesus got on the colt and rode it toward Jerusalem. Many people along the way laid their cloaks in the street so that the donkey could ride over them. This was a sign of great respect.

Others had cut palms and reeds in the field and they laid them in the street or waved them over their heads.

They all cried out, "Hosanna! Blessed is He who comes in the name of the Lord! Blessed is the reign of our father David to come! Hosanna in the highest!"

Hosanna is a word that means "Lord, help us."

When Jesus entered Jerusalem, the whole city was shaken. Many people heard the noise as the crowd cried out their greeting; so they were asking, "Who is this?"

The disciples of Jesus answered, "This is the prophet from Nazareth in Galilee."

When Jesus arrived at the temple, He was very disturbed by what He saw. There were people selling animals for the sacrifices that were to be performed that day in the temple. The people were shouting out their prices, and the animals were making all kinds of noise. It seemed more like a marketplace than a place where one could pray.

There were also money changers present. Most of the coins that the people had were Roman coins, and they had pictures of Roman gods on them. Therefore the people were not allowed to give them in the collection plate in the temple.

The money changers would exchange the Roman coins for Jewish coins that the pilgrims could give as an offering in the temple.

Jesus chased all the merchants and the money changers out of the temple. He cried out, "My house shall be called a house of prayer, but you have turned it into a den of thieves."

The priests and Pharisees were very angry when they heard what Jesus had done, and they plotted to have Him arrested and put to death.

The crowd cries Hosanna as Jesus enters Jerusalem.

Jesus washes the feet of His disciples.

THE LAST SUPPER: WASHING THE DISCIPLES' FEET

John 13:1-20

THE day before the feast of Passover, the disciples asked Jesus where He wanted to go to prepare the Passover meal. Jesus instructed two of them that they were to go into the city.

Jesus said, "You will come upon a man carrying a water jar. Follow him. Whatever house he enters, say to the owner, 'The Teacher asks, Where is My guest room where I may eat the Passover with My disciples?'

"Then he will show you an upper room spacious, furnished, and all in order. That is the place you are to get ready for us."

The disciples went off and found everything just as Jesus had told them. They prepared the room so that it would be ready for Jesus and the apostles when they arrived later on.

The feast of Passover began at sunset of that day, so they all gathered in the upper room just as the sun was about to set. They were going to eat a special meal to celebrate the fact that God had freed the people of Israel from their slavery in Egypt.

At the beginning of the meal, it was the custom for each person to wash in order to prepare for the special meal that was to follow. Jesus got up from the table and took off His cloak. He put a towel around His waist, took the water jar, and began to wash the feet of the apostles.

Peter was very upset when he saw what Jesus was doing. This was usually done by a servant, and here Jesus, their master and teacher, was doing it. When Jesus arrived at his place, Peter said that he did not want Jesus to wash his feet. But Jesus told Peter that if He did not wash his feet, then he could not enter the kingdom of God.

Peter then said that Jesus should wash his hands and his head as well, but Jesus told Peter that this was not necessary, for Peter was already clean. So Peter finally allowed Jesus to continue what He was doing.

When Jesus had finished washing their feet, He explained to them why He had done it. He said, "Do you understand what I just did for you?

"You call me 'Teacher' and 'Lord' and that is just, for that is what I am. But if I washed your feet, I who am Teacher and Lord, then you must wash each other's feet.

"What I just did was to give you an example: as I have done, so you must do."

"THIS IS MY BODY"

Matthew 26:26-29; Mark 14:22-25; Luke 22:15-20

JESUS and the others then began to eat the meal that had been prepared for their Passover celebration. They ate lamb just as the Israelites did before they left Egypt. They ate bitter herbs to remember their bitter years of slavery. They also ate bread and drank wine.

Jesus took some of the bread. He blessed it and broke it, giving it to His disciples. He said,

"Take this, all of you, and eat it. This is My body, which will be given up for you."

At the end of the meal, He took a cup of wine. He blessed it and gave it to His disciples, saying,

"Take this, all of you and drink it. This is the cup of My blood, the blood of the new and everlasting covenant. It will be shed for you so that sins may be forgiven. Do this in memory of Me."

Jesus gave this gift of His body and His blood to His apostles because He knew that He was going to die on the cross the next day. He wanted them to have a sign of His love. He also wanted to be with them and with us in a special way for all time.

To this day Christians take bread and wine and say the words of blessing over them that Jesus had said. When they break that bread and drink that wine, they are sharing in His body and His blood.

They are also promising that they will try to be as loving as God is. They will try to be bread that is broken to feed the hunger of many and wine that is poured out to satisfy their thirst.

Finally, this holy bread and wine is a promise that Jesus will be with us until He returns in His glory at the end of time.

One of the apostles did not eat the bread and wine that Jesus had blessed: Judas. He had already left the meal to betray Jesus.

At the end of the meal, Jesus told them that He would have to suffer and die and they would all run away. Peter was sure that he would never run away and he told Jesus that even if everyone else were to abandon Him, he would always stand by Him. Jesus told Peter that he, too, would run away. In fact, He said that before the rooster would crow the next morning, Peter would deny Him three times.

"This is My body; this is My blood."

Jesus prays in the garden of Gethsemane.

THE AGONY IN THE GARDEN

Matthew 26:36-42; Mark 14:32-42; Luke 22:39-46

WHEN the meal was over, Jesus and the disciples all sang a psalm to praise the Lord. Then they got up and left. Jesus led them across the valley to a garden where there were many olive trees.

Jesus left most of the disciples at the gate, but He brought Peter, James and John with Him as He entered the garden.

When they reached the middle of the garden, He told Peter, James, and John to remain where they were and pray while He went a little distance away from them to pray alone.

Jesus said, "My heart is filled with sorrow to the point of death. Remain here and stay awake."

However, it was already late at night. So the moment Jesus went off to pray, the disciples fell asleep.

Jesus walked a short distance away and fell down on His knees. He prayed to the Father, "My Father, if it is possible, let this cup pass Me by. Still, let it be as You would have it, not as I."

He was saying to His Father that He knew what would happen to Him the next day, how He would suffer and die.

Jesus was filled with fear and sadness. He did not want to have to undergo that suffering, and He prayed that it be done some other way if that were possible.

But Jesus also prayed that what He wanted was not as important as His following the will of the Father. He was putting Himself entirely in the Father's hands.

Jesus got up and went over to where He had left Peter, James, and John. He found them asleep and He said to Peter, "So you could not stay awake with Me for even an hour. Be on guard, and pray that you may not undergo the test. The spirit is willing, but the flesh is weak."

Peter had said that he was willing to die for Jesus, but he could not even stay awake for a little while to pray with Him.

Jesus returned to His prayer and once again asked the Father to take this cup of pain away. As before, Jesus said that if it was the Father's will for Him to suffer and die, He was willing to do it.

Again, Jesus got up and went over to His three disciples, who once again had fallen asleep.

Judas betrays Jesus with a kiss.

JUDAS BETRAYS JESUS

Matthew 26:47-56; Mark 14:43-52; Luke 22:47-53; John 18:2-12

JESUS went over a third time and prayed still again. When He had finished, He got up and found the apostles still asleep. This time He woke them up for His hour was now at hand. Judas, the apostle who had betrayed Him, and some soldiers were at the gate of the garden, for they had come to arrest Him.

Now Judas had been called to be an apostle just as the other eleven had been. He was the one who took care of the money for their food and their other needs.

At times Judas seems to have been too concerned with money, such as the time that Mary anointed Jesus' feet with an expensive perfume and Judas complained that the perfume should have been sold instead.

The priests and the Pharisees had been looking for a way to arrest Jesus. They were jealous of all the people who had followed Him and they were also afraid.

They had seen Jesus chase the merchants and the money changers out of the temple, and they were sure He would cause a riot. If He did, the Romans would come and they would make all the people suffer.

One day Judas visited the priests and offered to betray Jesus into their hands if they would pay him thirty pieces of silver. They agreed on that price, and Judas looked for an opportunity to hand Jesus over to them.

At the Last Supper, Jesus told the apostles that He knew one of them was going to betray Him. All of them tried to deny it, but Jesus sent Judas on his way to do what he had planned to do.

So Judas went off to tell the Jews that this was the right time, and he brought the soldiers with him to take Jesus away. He had arranged a sign with them that the one whom he kissed was the one they were to arrest.

Judas entered the garden and went over to Jesus and greeted Him with a kiss, saying, "Peace, Rabbi." Jesus asked him, "Judas, would you betray Me with a kiss?"

When the disciples saw what was happening, they tried to defend Jesus. Peter took out a sword and hit one of the men who had come with Judas. He cut off the ear of a man named Malchus who was a slave of the high priest. Jesus told Peter to put the sword away, for they were not to fight, and He healed the slave's ear.

Jesus asked the soldiers why they had come to arrest Him in the middle of the night when He had been in the temple every day and they had never arrested Him there.

Judas later felt such great guilt for what he had done that he killed himself.

THE TRIAL

Matthew 26:57—27:14; Mark 14:53—15:5; Luke 22:54—23:5; John 18:13-38

THE soldiers led Jesus off to the house of the high priest. There they questioned Him and tried to find a charge that they could hold against Him. They even hired two men to tell lies about what Jesus had said and done.

Finally, the high priest asked Jesus whether He was the Messiah. Jesus answered, "I am." This caused the high priest and all the others who were there to be filled with anger. They declared that this was blasphemy and they said that Jesus deserved to be put to death for saying this.

Yet, because of the laws of that land, they did not have the authority to put anyone to death. Only the Roman governor had that power. So they beat and mocked Jesus, and sent Him off to Pilate to be judged.

The disciple whom Jesus loved was trying to see what was happening. He knew the high priest and was able to get inside the courtyard of the high priest's house. He spoke with the woman at the gate and was able to get Peter inside the courtyard as well.

Peter stood warming himself by the fire there when one of the servant girls came up to him and said, "You too were with Jesus of Nazareth." Peter denied this, saying, "I do not know what you are talking about!"

The servant girl continued to tell people that she had seen Peter with Jesus, but once again Peter denied it.

Finally, one of the others warming himself at the fire said, "You are certainly one of them. You are a Galilean, are you not?" They could tell he came from Galilee by his accent.

Peter began to curse and said, "I do not even know the man you are talking about."

At that very moment, the rooster crowed and Peter remembered what Jesus had said. He was filled with guilt and sadness, and he wept.

They brought Jesus before Pilate, who asked them what the charge was. The Jews answered that they would not have brought Him there if He were not guilty.

Pilate asked Jesus, "Are You the king of the Jews?" Jesus answered, "Are you saying this on your own or have others been telling you about Me?" Pilate answered, "I am no Jew." So Jesus told him that He was a king, but His kingdom was not of this world.

At this Pilate said, "So, then, you are a king?" But Jesus told Pilate that He did not come into the world to receive a crown and throne, but only to give witness to the truth.

Pilate questions Jesus.

JESUS IS BEATEN

Matthew 27:15-31; Mark 15:6-20;
Luke 23:13-25; John 18:38—19:15

The soldiers torture Jesus.

PILATE now realized that Jesus was innocent, so he went out to speak to the crowd. He said that there was a custom that a prisoner was set free every Passover. At that time there was a dangerous murderer in prison named Barabbas. Pilate wanted to know whether they wanted to set Jesus free or Barabbas. He asked them this for he knew that they had handed over Jesus to him because they were jealous of Him.

Pilate did not want to have Jesus put to death. He knew in his heart that Jesus was innocent, and he had also received a message from his wife. She told him that she had had a dream about Jesus and that he should not allow them to kill Him.

The high priests and the elders of the Jews convinced the crowds that they should ask for Barabbas. So they cried out in a loud voice that they wanted him to set Barabbas free.

Pilate asked them what he should do with Jesus. They all cried out, "Crucify Him!" Pilate decided to have Jesus beaten by the soldiers in the hope that the crowd would be satisfied. So he sent Him off.

The soldiers beat Jesus badly. They took thorns and made them into a crown and put it on His head. They also took a purple robe and put it on Jesus. Then they mocked Jesus, kneeling before Him, saying, "All hail, king of the Jews." They spit at Him and slapped Him across the face.

When the soldiers had finished beating and mocking Jesus, they brought Him back before Pilate.

Pilate presents Jesus to the Jewish elders.

"BEHOLD THE MAN"

PILATE brought Jesus out to the crowd so they could see how badly He had been beaten. He proclaimed, "Behold the man." But as soon as the leaders of the crowd saw Him, they cried out, "Crucify Him! Crucify Him!" Pilate objected that He had done nothing wrong, but they responded that He had to die for He had claimed to be the Son of God.

Pilate spoke with Jesus again and asked Him where He came from. When Jesus did not answer, Pilate said to Him, "Do You not know I have the power to release You and the power to crucify You?" But Jesus answered him that his power was given to him by God.

The crowd began to cry out that if Pilate did not kill Jesus, then he would not be a friend of Caesar. At this Pilate had to act.

Pilate went out to his judgment seat. He washed his hands, saying that he was innocent of the blood of Jesus, for he knew that He was innocent. He then ordered Jesus to be taken away to be crucified.

Jesus falls under the weight of the cross.

JESUS CARRIES THE CROSS

Matthew 27:31-32; Mark 15:20-26; Luke 23:26-31; John 19:17

THE soldiers led Jesus out from the palace. They laid on His shoulders the wood of the cross and made Him carry it to the place where He was to die.

They also carried a sign that Pilate had ordered to be nailed to the cross for all to see. The sign said: "Jesus the Nazorean, king of the Jews."

It was written in Greek, Hebrew, and Latin so that all who passed by could read it no matter what language they spoke.

Some of the people complained that Pilate had made a mistake. He had proclaimed that Jesus was the king of the Jews, and not that He only claimed to be the king of the Jews. But when they approached Pilate with their complaint, he answered them saying, "What I have written, I have written."

As Jesus was carrying the cross, He met His mother. Her eyes were filled with the pain of a mother who was watching the death of her only child.

He also met a group of women who were weeping. He told them that they should not cry for Him, but rather for themselves and their children.

Jesus kept falling down, for He was very weak after all that they had done to Him. The soldiers began to worry that He might die before they reached the hill where He was to be nailed to the cross. They looked around for someone to help Jesus carry His cross.

A man named Simon of Cyrene was coming in from the fields and the soldiers stopped him as he was passing by. They forced him to carry the cross the rest of the way.

When the soldiers reached the hill called Golgotha, which means the place of the skull, they pulled off the robe that Jesus had been wearing. This hurt badly, for it caused all of Jesus' wounds to start to bleed again.

The soldiers then pushed Jesus down and nailed Him to the cross. They placed His cross between the crosses of two thieves.

The soldiers who were there would usually divide among themselves the garments of those who were being crucified. They noticed that Jesus' robe was made of a single piece of cloth and they realized that it would be ruined if they cut it, so they cast dice to see who would win it.

JESUS DIES ON THE CROSS

Matthew 27:33-66; Mark 15:22-47; Luke 23:33-56; John 19:17-42

IT was around nine in the morning when Jesus was nailed to the cross. He hung there until the middle of the afternoon.

Even the sky was filled with horror at what was happening to the Son of God. The sun became dark and there were great clouds and thunder and an earthquake.

One of the thieves who had been crucified with Jesus began to make fun of Him. But the other thief told him to stop.

He said, "Have you no fear of God, seeing you are under the same sentence? We are only paying the price for what we have done, but this man has done nothing wrong."

Then he said, "Jesus, remember me when You come into Your kingdom."

Jesus then turned His head to the good thief and promised him, "I assure you, this day you will be with Me in paradise."

Many of those who passed by also made fun of Jesus. They cried out, "So You are the one who was going to destroy the temple and rebuild it in three days. Save Yourself, why don't You? Come down off that cross if You are God's Son."

Jesus did not respond to their mockery. Instead He prayed, "Father, forgive them; they do not know what they are doing."

Later on He prayed the first line of a psalm, "My God, My God, why have You forsaken Me." This psalm, which begins without hope, ends with the promise that God will deliver His faithful one.

Some of the soldiers noticed that Jesus was thirsty, so one ran off and brought some wine that he put on a sponge and raised to Jesus' lips. Jesus refused to drink it.

The mother of Jesus and the disciple whom Jesus loved were standing below the cross. Jesus looked down at His mother and said, "Woman, behold your son," and to the beloved disciple He said, "Behold your mother." From that time on the beloved disciple cared for Mary.

When all was finished, Jesus cried out, "Father, into Your hands I commend My spirit," and He breathed His last.

A soldier came up to break the legs of those who were on the crosses so that they would die faster, but when he came to Jesus, he saw that He was already dead. The soldier pierced His side with a lance, and immediately blood and water flowed out.

Joseph of Arimathea, a secret disciple of Jesus, asked Pilate for the body. Then in the presence of His mother and the ministering women, he took the body of Jesus down from the cross and buried it in a tomb that was found in a garden nearby.

Jesus commends His spirit into the hands of the Father.

Jesus rises from the dead.

EASTER SUNDAY

Matthew 28:1-10; Mark 16:1-20; Luke 24:1-12; John 20:1-23

EARLY on Sunday morning, some women went out to the tomb with oil and perfume to anoint the body of Jesus.

They had not had time to do this on Friday after Jesus had died, for it had been sunset of the holy day and the body of Jesus had to be buried in a hurry.

As they went along, they asked among themselves how they were going to get into the tomb for the Jews had placed a huge rock in front of its entrance.

When they arrived at the tomb, they were surprised to see that the rock had already been rolled back. They leaned into the tomb and there they found a young man dressed in a white robe, an angel.

They were filled with fear, but he told them, "You need not be amazed. You are looking for Jesus of Nazareth, the One who was crucified. He has been raised up. He is not here. See the place where they laid Him. Go now and tell His disciples and Peter, 'He is going ahead of you to Galilee, where you will see Him just as He told you.' "

Peter and the beloved disciple heard the report of the women that Jesus had been raised from the dead; so they ran as fast as they could to see for themselves. The beloved disciple reached the tomb first, but he did not enter. He waited for Peter who went into the tomb.

Peter and John found the wrappings with which Jesus had been buried, but there was no body. And so the disciples went back home.

Meanwhile, Mary Magdalene stood by the tomb weeping. She did not understand yet what had happened, and she thought that someone had stolen Jesus' body.

Mary went inside the tomb and saw two angels sitting inside. They asked her, "Woman, why are you weeping?" She answered, "Because the Lord has been taken away, and I do not know where they have put Him."

She saw a man walking in the garden and she presumed him to be the gardener. He asked her, "Woman, why are you weeping? Who is it you are looking for?"

She ran up to him and said, "Sir, if you are the one who carried Him off, tell me where you have laid Him and I will take Him away." Jesus said to her, "Mary." She recognized Him and said, "Rabboni," which means teacher.

Jesus then told Mary not to cling to Him, for He had not yet ascended to the Father. He sent her to go to the disciples to proclaim that He had risen from the dead.

Jesus speaks with the two disciples on the road to Emmaus.

THE ROAD TO EMMAUS

Mark 16:12-13; Luke 24:13-35

THAT same day, the first day of the week, two of Jesus' disciples were walking from Jerusalem to Emmaus, a village about seven miles away.

They were very disturbed, for they did not really understand why Jesus had to die. Then earlier that day they had heard a report that Jesus had risen from the dead, but they did not know what to make of it.

They were discussing all of this along the way when a man approached them and joined in their conversation. The man who was speaking with them was Jesus, but they did not recognize Him. He asked them what they were discussing along the way.

One of them stopped and looked at Jesus in disbelief and asked Him, "Are You the only resident of Jerusalem who does not know the things that went on there these past few days?"

He said, "What things?"

They answered, "All those things that had to do with Jesus of Nazareth, a prophet powerful in word and deed in the eyes of God and all the people; how our chief priests and leaders delivered Him up to be condemned to death, and crucified Him.

"We were hoping that He was the one who would set Israel free. Besides all this, today, the third day since these things happened, some women of our group have just brought us some astonishing news.

"They were at the tomb before dawn and failed to find His body, but returned with the tale that they had seen a vision of angels who declared He was alive. Some of our number went to the tomb and found it to be just as the women said, but Him they did not see."

Jesus spoke to them and explained that all these things had been predicted by the prophets. He then went all through the Old Testament and showed them how the law and the prophets had foretold that all of these things had to happen.

In the evening the two disciples decided to stop where they were for the night. They invited Jesus to remain with them.

When they sat down to eat, Jesus took the bread, blessed it and broke it, giving it to them. At that moment they recognized that it was Jesus, and He disappeared from their sight.

They said to each other, "Did not our hearts burn with love as we walked along with Him?" Then they ran back to Jerusalem to tell the others what had happened.

When they arrived, they were greeted with the message, "The Lord has been raised! It is true! He has appeared to Simon."

Jesus invites Thomas to touch His hands, feet, and side.

DOUBTING THOMAS

John 20:19-29

THE apostles were all gathered in the upper room the evening of the day that Jesus had been raised from the dead. This was the room in which they had celebrated the Last Supper. They had locked the door for fear of the Jews.

Jesus passed through the locked door and said to them, "Peace be with you." He showed them the marks in His hands, feet, and side. The disciples were filled with joy when they saw Him and heard His greeting. He then said again, "Peace be with you."

The Lord went over to the disciples and breathed on them. He told them, "Receive the Holy Spirit. If you forgive people's sins, they are forgiven them; if you hold them bound, they are held bound."

One of the apostles, Thomas, was not there when Jesus appeared to the others on Easter Sunday. He told the others that he would not believe that

Jesus had been raised from the dead until he could touch the hands and the feet of Jesus where the nails had been and touch the side of Jesus that had been wounded by the lance.

The next Sunday the disciples were gathered together again and Thomas was present there this time. Once again the doors were locked and Jesus passed through the door. He extended a greeting of peace to them.

Then Jesus said to Thomas, "Take your finger and examine My hands. Put your finger in My side. Do not persist in your unbelief, but believe."

Thomas now knew that this was truly Jesus who had risen from the dead and he said, "My Lord and my God."

Jesus said to him, "You became a believer because you saw Me. Blessed are they who have not seen and have believed."

Jesus was speaking of each one of us who have come to believe in Jesus even though we have not seen Him with our eyes.

The Lord wanted to make sure the apostles understood what had happened. When He first appeared to them, some of them thought He was a ghost.

Jesus said to them, "Why are you disturbed? Why do such ideas cross your mind? Look at My hands and My feet; it is really I. Touch Me, and see that a ghost does not have flesh and bones as I do."

Jesus then ate some cooked fish to show the apostles that He was not a ghost.

Finally, when they understood that He had risen, Jesus explained to them about all those things that the prophets had said about Him. He opened their minds to the understanding of the Bible.

He told them, "Thus it is written that the Messiah must suffer and rise from the dead on the third day." They were to preach the forgiveness of sins to people in Jerusalem and all around the world.

Jesus also promised them that He would send the Holy Spirit down upon them to fill them with the power of God.

Still another time the Lord appeared to the apostles in Galilee. When they saw Him, they fell down and paid Him homage.

Jesus told them that He was giving them the very power of God. He told them to go out to the nations and baptize all peoples.

They were to baptize them in the name of the Father, and of the Son, and of the Holy Spirit.

Jesus also promised them that He would never leave them. He would be with them until the end of time.

Jesus asks Peter to care for His sheep.

"PETER, DO YOU LOVE ME?"

John 21:1-19

SOME of the disciples, Peter, Thomas, Nathanael, James, and John and a few others, went out to the Sea of Galilee. Peter told them, "I am going out to fish," and the others agreed to join him. They fished all night but were unable to catch anything.

Around daybreak, Jesus appeared to them standing on the shore, but they did not recognize that it was He. He called out to them and asked whether they had caught anything, and they answered that they had not.

So Jesus suggested that they cast their nets off the right side of the boat and they might catch something.

The disciples tossed the nets in again on the right side of the boat. When they pulled their nets up, they discovered that they had made a huge catch of fish. The disciple whom Jesus loved then realized that it was Jesus standing on the shore and he cried out, "It is the Lord!" Peter, too, realized that it was Jesus standing on the shore so he threw on his clothes and jumped into the water.

Meanwhile, the other disciples pulled in to shore. They counted the fish in the net, and there were one hundred and fifty-three large fish in all.

Jesus had prepared some breakfast for the disciples to eat. He told the disciples to bring some of the freshly caught fish over, and He prepared these as well.

When they had finished eating, Jesus asked Peter, "Simon, son of John, do you love Me more than these?" He answered, "Yes, Lord." So Jesus told him, "Feed My lambs."

Jesus asked Peter a second time, "Simon, son of John, do you love Me?" Peter answered, "Yes, Lord, You know that I love You."

A third time Jesus asked Peter, "Simon, son of John, do you love Me?" Peter felt bad, for he knew that Jesus had asked him three times whether he loved Him because Peter had denied Him three times.

Peter replied, "Lord, You know everything. You know well that I love You." So Jesus told Him, "Feed My sheep."

Jesus had asked Peter if he loved Him and He had told him to take care of His flock because he was asking Peter to care for His Church.

Peter was to be the shepherd of the Church for he was to show it as much love as Jesus, the Good Shepherd, had shown to him and the other disciples.

PENTECOST

Acts 1:1—2:47

JESUS continued to appear to the apostles for many days after He had been raised from the dead. Forty days after the resurrection, He and the disciples were on a hillside outside Jerusalem. He blessed them and told them to go back to Jerusalem to wait for the fulfillment of the Father's promise to send the Spirit upon them. Then He was lifted up into the clouds.

There He sits at the right hand of the Father for all time.

Ten days later the apostles and Mary were gathered in the upper room to pray. Suddenly, they heard a loud noise like a strong wind. When they looked around, they saw that there were small flames of fire over the heads of each one of them.

The wind and the fire were signs that the Holy Spirit had come upon them to fill them with God's life in a special way.

Now there were many people in Jerusalem who had come up to celebrate the feast of Pentecost, a feast celebrated fifty days after Passover. There were Jews from all over the world, and they spoke many different languages. Yet, when Peter, filled with the courage of the Holy Spirit, came out to speak to them about Jesus and all He had done for them, they could all understand him as if he were speaking in their own language.

At first they thought that he and the others were drunk, for they were filled with the Holy Spirit. As they listened to the words of Peter, they realized that this was not the case.

Peter told them that Jesus was the answer to the promises that God had made to His people all throughout the Old Testament. He spoke of how Jesus had worked miracles and signs and wonders filled with the power of God, but how their leaders had put Him to death.

Yet God would not allow death to defeat Jesus, for God raised Him from the dead.

Now God had sent His Spirit upon the followers of Jesus so that they could be a new Israel, one that was free from sin.

Many of the people in the crowd listened to what Peter had to say. They were deeply moved, and when Peter invited them to come forward and to be baptized, some three thousand of them decided to do so.

Jesus' followers came to be called Christians and tried to live the message that Jesus had proclaimed to them. They shared everything they had with each other and no one suffered any need.

All who saw them could only say of them, "See how much these Christians love each other."

The Holy Spirit descends upon Mary and the apostles.

AFTERWORD

WHEN we read the stories of the Bible, we are filled with wonder at all of the wonderful things God has done for us.

In the Old Testament, God called a people and made a covenant with them. He protected them, corrected them, guided them, and most of all loved them.

Then in the New Testament, Jesus invited all peoples to enter into His holy covenant. He taught us His ways through words and example. Then He gave us the greatest sign of His love when He died on the cross.

As we read about these stories, we are also being called to be part of God's holy people. All of us are invited to ask ourselves what it means to be a Christian, a follower of Christ. We are asked to turn away from our sins and selfishness and from anything else that might keep us away from Christ. We are asked to commit ourselves to Christ in love.

Finally, this following of Christ must be done in our everyday lives. It is not enough to say that we love God and then do whatever we want. We must follow the example of these holy men and women about whom we have read.

We must show our parents, brothers and sisters, friends, teachers and anyone else we meet the same love that God has shown to us. When we do that, everyone will know that we are disciples of Jesus, and our lives will become stories of people who love God.

OTHER OUTSTANDING CATHOLIC BOOKS

HOLY BIBLE—Saint Joseph Edition of the completely modern translation called the New American Bible. Printed in large type with helpful Notes and Maps, Photographs, Family Record Pages and Bible Dictionary. **Family Edition**   **Ask for No. 612**
Large Size Edition   **Ask for No. 611**
Medium Size Edition   **Ask for No. 609**
Giant Print Edition   **Ask for No. 616**
Personal Size Edition   **Ask for No. 510**

BIBLE MEDITATIONS FOR EVERY DAY—By Rev. John Kersten, S.V.D. Excellent aid for daily meditation on the Word of God. A scripture passage and a short invaluable introduction are given for every day of the year. The author deals with themes relevant to today's living and thus brings the faith home to his readers.   **Ask for No. 277**

NEW TESTAMENT—St. Joseph Edition of the New American Bible Version. Large easy-to-read type, with helpful Notes and Maps. Photographs, and Study Guide. 432 pages. **Study Edition**   **Ask for No. 311**
Pocket Size Edition—legible type . Illustrated   **Ask for No. 630**
Giant Type Edition—Illustrated.   **Ask for No. 312**

PICTURE BOOK OF SAINTS—By Rev. L. Lovasik, S.V.D. Illustrated Lives of the Saints in **full color** for Young and Old. It clearly depicts the lives of over 100 popular Saints in word and picture.   **Ask for No. 235**

MY FIRST PRAYERBOOK—By Rev. Lawrence G. Lovasik, S.V.D. Beautiful new prayerbook that provides prayers for the main occasions in a child's life. Features simple language, easy-to-read type, and full-color illustrations.   **Ask for No. 205**

THE MASS FOR CHILDREN—By Rev. Jude Winkler, OFM Conv. New beautifully illustrated Mass Book that explains the Mass to children and contains the Mass responses they should know. It is sure to help children know and love the Mass.   **Ask for No. 215**

LIVES OF THE SAINTS—**New Revised Edition.** Short life of a Saint and prayer for every day of the year. Over 50 illustrations. Ideal for daily meditation and private study.   **Ask for No. 870**

GREAT PEOPLE OF THE BIBLE—By Rev. Jude Winkler, O.F.M., Conv. Full-page portrait of more than 70 biblical personages accompanied by a concise one-page biography.   **Ask for No. 485**

WHEREVER CATHOLIC BOOKS ARE SOLD